AF579189

Pictorial History of the FRENCH AIR FORCE

VOLUME 2

In March 1963 the escadron 3/33 Moselle started conversion at Mont de Marsan on the Dassault Mirage IIIR, the reconnaissance version of the Mirage IIIC then in service. Six months later it was operational on the type it has operated ever since from Strasbourg-Entzheim. Bearing the c/n 315, this aircraft sports the squadron emblem on the fin, instead of on the fuselage as was customary on its RF-84F.

Pictorial History of the FRENCH AIR FORCE

VOLUME 2
1941~1974

André Van Haute

LONDON

IAN ALLAN LTD

Contents

First published 1975

ISBN 0 7110 0595 8-98/75

Published by Ian Allan Ltd, Shepperton, Surrey, and printed and bound in the United Kingdom by R. J. Acford Ltd., Chichester, Sussex.

The Dassault Mystere II was a straightforward development of the Duragan, with 30 degree swept wings. It was the first operational French design to have swept wings, via the Mystere I which remained non-operational. A pre-production aircraft, c/n 05 is depicted here.

1 | *The Battle of France*

Prelude to *The Onslaught*

As related in volume one, the Armée de l'Air was in progress of receiving new equipment for both its offensive and defensive units at the end of the 'phoney war'.

What was its situation on the eve of the German offensive of May 10th, 1940?

Operating for the various armies in the field, the air force operational commands were divided in zones according to the armies they had to protect or support. They were the northern, eastern and southern zones and the zone of the Alpine region. These zones were known respectively as ZOAN (Zone d'Opérations Aériennes Nord) ZOAE (East) ZOAS (South) and ZOAA (Alpine region). Fighter elements had been divided into Groups or what was known to the French as Groupements. These comprised Groupements 21, 25 and 23 whose mission was to protect respectively Paris and the lower Seine region, Dunkirk and the Belgian frontier, along which the VII Army was posted, and the II and IX Armies along the Belgo-Luxemburg border. As for Groupements 22 and 24, these were charged with protecting the remaining borders with Germany.

Each Groupement had a certain number of Groupes de Chasse (GC) under its command. Statutory strength of these varied from 20 to 34 aircraft but out of a force of 571 fighter aircraft 421 were available including 28 Potez 631 night fighters. A further 94 fighters belonging to four Groupes de Chasse, and including the first 60 operational Dewoitine D-520s were also ready for action. These figures did not of course include aircraft based overseas, nor such types as the Dutch Koolhoven FK-58 nor Caudron-Renault 'Cyclone' CR.714, the former being judged totally unsuitable for the job, and the latter in the process of equipping a Polish-manned GCI/145.

Bomber elements assigned to the operation zones were as follows: Groupements de Bombardement 6 and 9 comprising four Groupes de Bombardement (GB) and Groupement 18 with two of the crack Groupes de Bombardement d'Attaque (GBA) equipped with Breguet 693s belonging to the ZOAN and under the command of the Ire Division Aérienne (1st Air Div) with HQ at Laon. This air division also had under its control the fighter and reconnaissance aircraft assigned to the particular zone.

As for the ZOAE, this zone could muster two Groupements de Bombardement, Nos 10 and 15 respectively, which came under command of the 3e Division Aérienne (3rd Air Div) with headquarters at Vitry Le Francois.

At the outbreak of the Battle of France on May 10th, 1940, ten out of twenty-three groupes de chasse were still equipped with the Morane 406 fighter. Note the camouflage scheme of these factory fresh M.S. 406s ready for take off.

By far the biggest consumer of bomber groups was the ZOAA which, according to RAF standards, could be considered as a big OCU and OTU alike. It was there that bomber squadrons re-equipped with new types, made their conversion training and where newly-formed crews got their training at the Groupement d'Instruction de l'Aviation de Bombardement du Sud-Est or GIABSE. In addition, ZOAA could muster the Groupements de Bombardement Nos 1, 7, 9, 11, 19 and part of Groupement de Bombardement 6, some of its units being in fact assigned to the ZOAN.

Transposed in numbers of aircraft available for immediate operations, this gave unfortunately the following result: out of a total of 400 bombers only 210 were modern types, the remaining 190 being obsolete, some obsolescent. However, even the 210 modern types couldn't even be accounted for as a means of retaliation as 13 of the available Amiot 354 bombers were not yet completely equipped to be fully operational. If one knows the industrial potential of France and the inborn ingenuity of some of its inhabitants one can only guess what the front line pilots must have thought about some of the senior ranks responsible for such a mess, taking into account that a so called 'phoney war' had been going on. The same thing applied to the 26 Glenn Martin 167s (RAF Maryland). As a matter of fact, only 54 out of 94 Lioré et Olivier Léo-451 bombers were available, together with 31 out of 35 Breguet Br-693 assault bombers. All—but all—the remaining bombers were either destined for conversion training and not available on the front line, or either obsolete types just good enough for night operations.

Eleven out of the 22 Potez 633 and 14 out of the 19 Breguet 691 assault bombers available served at OTUs, whilst six long range Farman F-221/222s out of 21 at strength, and numbers of Bloch 200/210s and Amiot 143s made up the remnants. Reconnaissance and observation aircraft accounted for roughly the same numbers available as the bombers, if one counted only the modern types. If the more obsolete were added, figures rose accordingly. The most popular was certainly the Potez 63.11, of which not less than 238 were available, and over 150 in maintenance, etc. Out of a total of 39 of the superior Bloch MB.174 taken on strength by the Armée de l'Air at that date, 24 were available with recce groups and another eight did test duties at various experimental establishments.

19 Potez 637s accounted for the bulk of modern aircraft, whilst 25 Bloch 131s, 53 Mureaux 115s and another 34 Mureaux 117s made up the better part of the immediately available second line recce planes, which were available to the armies at the front. In contrast to what exists nowadays, there were extremely few transport aircraft available to back up this force. Indeed, when France went to war in September 1939, the only known transport units were the Potez 650s of the GIA I/601 and I/602 as illustrated in volume one. These aircraft were destined to transport the parachute troops of the Détachements d'Infanterie de l'Air Nos 601 and 602, formed in 1937 and presently (1940) stationed at Montélimar and Pujaut. These units never operated as paratroopers during the conflict, and were rather used as were 'Commandos' later on with the British army.

Of the large number of civilian transport aircraft in service all over the country, a number were impressed to form the Groupement Aérien de Transport, a forerunner of the present CoTAM. This GAT had four sections known as SAT 1, 5, 8 and 9, and were equipped with Wibault 283 twin-engined transports. These units flew support missions for both the Armée de l'Air, Army and RAF. Later on each section was put at the disposal of a ZOA (Zone Aérienne).

Besides ex-civilian aircraft, the air staff had, albeit a bit late, ordered different types of transport aircraft for the Armée de l'Air. Amongst them were four-engined Farman F-224s, Caudron C-445s, etc. Bloch 220s equipped the GAT I/444 (Groupement Aérien de Transport). Of the two original transport units I/601 and I/602, the former was the recipient during May 1940 of five of the above Farman F-224 heavy transports, some of its own Potez 650s going to its sister squadron I/602 as complement. For long-range flights there were at least five Sections d'Avions Long Courrier (SALC I/110—303/139, 304/139, 305/139 and 306/139) each of which had three of the excellent Dewoitine D-338 three-engined transports. Other units which existed in some numbers were the medical evacuation flights (Section Aérienne Sanitaire or SAS) with such aircraft as Bloch-81 SAN or impressed civilian planes, the liaison flights or Section d'Avions Estafette, at least twenty formed, with Potez P-585s, Caudron C-635s, etc. and the ten light transport flights (Section d'Avions de Transport Léger or SAT) with impressed Wibault 282s and 283s and Caudron C-445 Goëland. Even the prototype of the new four-engined Bloch 160 transport was impressed.

No air force can exist without the backing of a sound training organization. The Armée de l'Air had been well aware of this in the past, but

Such had been the need for training aircraft in the mid-thirties, that the French had to look outside their own country for some of their requirements. From Italy they bought various types, amongst them 182 Romano Ro-82 biplanes of which c/n 21 is illustrated. Note the paint-job, the front part of the fuselage being in silver-grey paint, the rest in drab finish.

with the ever-increasing demand for personnel with the start of World War II there was also an increasing requirement for more advanced trainers. What then was its situation at the start of the 'Blitzkrieg'? Primary and basic training had been catered for long before the outbreak of war, thanks to the procurement programmes of the early thirties which accounted for large orders of the Morane Saulnier MS-230 and MS-315 (500 and 239 respectively), Hanriot H-182 and Romeo Ro-82. Not all of these had been delivered by May 10th, but on the other hand quantities of impressed civilian trainers and club aircraft balanced this out.

Basic training had been a quite different problem as far as new aircraft procurement was concerned, especially for those pilots destined for the fighter arm. Luckily enough, the North American Aircraft Corporation, on the other side of the Atlantic, had already gained a certain good name with its BT-9 basic trainer. This forerunner of the T-6 Harvard (or Texan) was thus ordered in large numbers. Not less than 230, together with 345 engines, were bought by contract 652/9 in February 1939, whilst a repeat order on October 10th numbered 230 aircraft and 275 engines. The first four NAA-57s, as the BT-9 was known by the French, arrived in crates early in August 1939 to be assembled by the SNCA-Ouest at Nantes. 128 were to reach France before January 1940 and thus served before the German offensive in the west. Another 40 were sent straight to Morocco in December 1939 and ten the following May. The flying training schools of Etampes, Avord, Salon de Provence home of the Ecole de l'Air (equivalent of the RAF College, Cranwell) and Saint-Cyr were amongst the recipients of the NAA-57. In addition to this very modern trainer for its day, the Armée de l'Air had at least 110 Caudron C-635 Simoun aircraft, which, although not exactly designed exclusively as training aircraft (numbers served in the liaison and communications role) did their job very well. (This figure does not include the impressed civilian types which served the SAE (Section d'Avions Estafette).)

For the multi-engined conversion, the Caudron C-445M 'Goëland' was well suited but unfortunately there were not enough available. To supplement this, no fewer than 200 Italian Caproni Ca-313 twin-engined bomber/trainers were ordered. A development of the well known Ca-309 'Ghibli', in service overseas with the Regia Aeronautica, this type of aircraft was intended to supplement the Breguet Br-691 assault bomber/trainer. As a matter of fact, it proved itself completely unsuitable for this sort of mission. The home-built Hanriot H-232 destined for the same role was a quite different aircraft, but for various reasons, only 32 of the 55 ordered were to reach the air force before the final onslaught.

Whilst on the subject of foreign equipment for the air force training command, it is interesting to know that two other types of Italian aircraft served with the Armée de l'Air. 100 Caproni Ca-164 biplanes were ordered. These too were delivered in crates, and assembly took place at the SNCASE works at Marseille-Marignane. 49 were on strength on 10th May, 1940. At least 36 Nardi Fn-305 fighter trainers were also delivered, but little is known about them. The aerodrome of Cannes-Mandelieu on the Riviera saw their passage, and this particular type of aircraft saw service with the Italian and other air forces. Its speed, retractable undercarriage and 7.5mm MG made it a suitable trainer for fighter pilots of its day .

Some sources state also that the French ordered a certain number of North American NAA-64 basic trainers but although the well-known French periodical *Aviation Magazine* published a picture of such a NAA-64, and traces have been found of a German wartime picture showing ac. with s/n 44 and Luftwaffe markings, no trace has yet been found of the original order, nor quantities delivered. As far as the

The Caudron Goeland twin engined light transport saw considerable service prior to, during, and after the second world war, many being built for the Luftwaffe during the Occupation. Three hundred and twenty were built for French forces after the war in various versions depending on the type of engines, most of them going to the AA.

operational conversion units were concerned, there had been a lesser demand for new types, as aircraft such as the Dewoitine D-500/510, etc, served in this role. In general, former first-line bombers and fighters served in this conversion role.

This then, was the canvas which the Luftwaffe intended to smash to a shambles on this fateful day in May 1940.

The Onslaught

05.35hr. German time, May 10, 1940. From the Dutch border to the Maginot Line three Army Groups (Heeresgruppe A, B and C), comprising ten Panzerdivisionen, one Luft-Lande Korps (Airborne Corps) and several infantry and motorized divisions had started their attack towards France and the Low Countries. In support of this, they had the might of two Luftflotten (Luftflotte 2 under Kesselring and Luftflotte 3 under Sperrle) with a nominal strength of 3,634 aircraft, 1,016 fighters, 1,562 bombers, 501 long and short range reconnaissance aircraft and 555 other types, comprising mostly transports of the Ju-52/3m type and DFS230 assault gliders. Using tactics applied with success during the Polish campaign, their aim was to wipe out the allied air forces on the ground from the very start of the campaign.

In the air *en route* to their targets at dawn they expected to find the French fighters as sitting ducks. A somewhat different sort of reception committee was often waiting for them.

At Laon-Chambry, the CO of the Groupe de Chasse II/2 just had time to jump aboard his Morane 406, less helmet and parachute, when a formation of Do-17s attacked the field. Joining a second formation of Do-17s in the course of bombing the Laon station, he slowly succeeded in approaching a section of three, opening fire at point blank range. With one engine on fire, a German bomber went down, but the Morane had also been hit under the crossfire of the enemy formation. With oil covering his windshield, Commandant Bertrou crash-landed at his base. In the meantime, the pilots at readiness had also taken off, once the bombs were dropped on the field, and they intercepted the Germans on their way back.

At Suippes a first patrol on alert had taken off at 04.45hr. Two Curtiss Hawks, flown by two young NCOs had been ordered to patrol between 4,000 and 7,000m to protect their base. Unfortunately, one Curtiss had to return with engine trouble whilst the one piloted by Sergent-Chef Morel went on. At 6,000m contact was suddenly made with a formation of Me-110s. Opening fire on the left wingman, the latter plunged earthwards, but the other Me-110s fully intended to avenge their comrade and with controls partially jammed, Morel escaped only by diving towards the earth.

In the meantime, at 04.55hr another patrol led by Captain Accart and a Czech sergeant made contact with a mixed formation of Do-17s and Me-110 escorts at about 6,000m over Verdun. With no positive result for this show, they joined another formation of three Curtiss Hawks of their unit which had a row with some unescorted bombers. A Do-17 fell victim to Accart and his wingman's guns, whilst the other three pilots of GCI/5 succeeded in bringing down another one which force-landed. However, the enemy gunners had badly mauled Lt Rey's aircraft, whilst Lt Goupy, badly wounded in the thigh, landed his fighter at another base. At Xaffevillers, home of the GCII/4 equipped with Curtiss Hawks, things were slightly different. Thick fog prevented the French from taking off, but with past experience of the phoney war in mind, the Germans intended to destroy the aircraft of GCII/4. At least 50 bombs came down on the airfield and its vicinity and six Curtiss Hawks were written off.

At Toul-Croix de Metz, home of the GCII/5, dawn was appearing when a recce Do-17 approached the town, turning around without much bother from the local anti-aircraft guns. Commandant Hugues's pilots, nine of whom were at readiness as usual in this unit, waited for the van to carry them to their Curtiss Hawks. Unfortunately, Groupement 22 at Metz, from whom they should have received orders, apparently forgot to send them into the air.

It was a good thing that the aircraft were hidden in pens on the perimeter of the aerodrome, because suddenly a formation of He-111s appeared low over the field. With everybody dashing for cover, and bombs bursting all over, two of the pilots nearest the Hawks ran towards their aircraft. With mechanics standing by, and the engines previously having been warmed up as routine, they strapped themselves in and were off. Lt Ruchoux's Curtiss was not yet off the ground when the Heinkels made their second pass. With the engine at full power he managed to get into the air before bombs were exploding again on the field. His wingman, Sgt Hème had less luck and, seen from the place where the other pilots had taken shelter, it appeared that his Curtiss Hawk was enclosed by a wall of fire. Thirty seconds later, however, he emerged from the flames and, joining Lt Ruchoux, they were on the tail of the Germans who, apparently unaware of what was coming up, continued their formation flying as if on parade. Climbing up to 3,000m they dived on the enemy formation out of the sun. Each pilot took the outer Heinkels in his sight, coming as near as possible. Ruchoux opened fire at about 150m, trying to avoid the slipstream of his opponent. With its port engine on fire, the bomber gradually lost altitude and soon the crew was seen to jump out by parachute. As for Sgt Hème, he too shot down his He-111. Back at base, both pilots got a reprimand from their CO for having taken off without authority. It appeared that Group HQ had wanted all the II/5 Curtiss Hawks available for the day's end. The story goes that Ruchoux pointed out to his CO that, where his Curtiss had been standing, a bomb had exploded anyway, and that now his fighter was still in one piece.

That the Luftwaffe had planned to catch the allies unaware was again well proved, judging from the official German time of the attacks on the Low Countries, it was at 04.00hr. that a German bomber appeared at Norrent-Fontes to attack the Moranes of GCIII/1. When the Germans came back some minutes later *en force* with several He-111s, the remaining Morane 406 fighters managed to destroy several of them. Amongst the pilots taking part in this operation were a certain Sgt Durand and Warrant Officer (Adjudant) Déchanet, neither of whom would have believed that he would avenge this and other attacks to follow, far away in the Soviet Union, years later. In the meantime, their next posting was only across the border to Moerbeke-Waas near Gent in Belgium, where GCIII/1 had arrived. If, as related in these few anecdotes, the fighter arm had reacted relatively well towards the German attacks, it was a

Fine air view of a Curtiss Hawk H.75 which saw service with the Armée de l'Air in various versions ranging from the A-1 to the A-4. The most popular version being the A-3 with superior armament to the A-1 and A-2 versions and slightly better take off horse power. Out of a total of 316 aircraft taken on charge in France, six were of the A-4 sub type. Another thirty were sunk on board the vessel *Champlain* in La Rochelle harbour by Luftwaffe action and 23 of the A-4 version were left for over two years to rot away at Guadeloupe and Martinique in the West Indies.

quite different matter as far as the bomber and reconnaissance units were concerned, and this for obvious reasons. Not all of the 30 plus aerodromes which had been honoured by a Luftwaffe visit had been able to send some fighters into the air to reciprocate and the Armée de l'Air had very few of the very good Hotchkiss 25mm guns for its local aerodrome defence. The GAO (Groupes Aériens d'Observations) and the GR (Groupes de Reconnaissance) were amongst the first victims. Rather near the front line, some were surprised by attack in the early morning, whilst others received their share in the course of the day. No real air raid warning system existed, telephone communications were often non existent, or came too late, and there was of course no radar on this side of the Channel. GAO2/551 lost all his aircraft during a single air raid. GAO4/551 lost six out of nine Potez 63 11s during a surprise attack at 04.55hr. The crack GRII/33 based at Monceau le Waast was in its turn attacked by Do-17s around 05.30hr. One of the first units to re-equip with the Bloch 174, it lost one such aircraft (s/n 47) together with a Potez 63-11 (s/n 154) whilst two other Potez 63-11s were slightly damaged. The list could go on. The next day, May 11th, French bomber elements were requested to intervene on the Albert Kanaal in Belgium. Once considered Belgium's main line of defence, this waterway had been crossed by German forces from the first day of the offensive. As for the bridges over this canal and the river Maas in the Maastricht region, they were the main worry of Germans and allies alike. For the former their destruction meant a dangerous bottleneck for their advancing panzer and motorized columns, and for the latter they had to be destroyed at whatever cost to halt the German advance. Two French bomber groups of Groupement 6 were at first chosen for the job as far as the Armée de l'Air was concerned, GBII/12 stationed at Persan-Beaumont, equipped with Lioré Olivier 451s and

Breguet 693 of GBA 1/51. During the whole period of the 'Battle of France' these units equipped with Br 693 such as GBA 1/51, 11/51, 1/54, 11/54 and 11/35 fought well and achieved good results with few losses, the one exception being the mauling they received during the May 11th attack on the bridges over the Albert Canal in Belgium. Note individual a/c number in roman characters.

GBI/12 stationed at Soissons-Saconin. A morning mission was flown by 12 bombers, escorted by 18 Morane 406s from GCII/6. Jumped by Me-109s near their target, the French escort fighters managed to keep the Germans from the Léo. 451s but these were taken under such heavy fire from the amassed flak near the bridges, that one bomber was touched and had to crash-land on return to base, whilst the others, thanks to the sturdiness of their construction, were able to reach their bases. Unfortunately, the bridges remained undamaged In the afternoon another six bombers of the same units tried again, with escorts from both GCII/6 and III/3. One bridge was slightly damaged the remaining two being unscathed. This time the French escorting fighters lost some of their number during dogfights with a large formation of Me-109s. Flying a recce mission for a French motorized division, a Potez 63-11 of the GAO545 was jumped upon by not less than eight Messerschmitt 109s and shot down. Another Potez 63-11 belonging to the GRI/36 was touched by flak during a low level mission over La Blies. Trying to open his canopy, the observer fell out of the plane towards the enemy lines, but the aircraft was brought back safely by its pilot. On May 12th the High Command again brought forward the problem of the bridges over the Albert Kanaal. A Potez 637, flying a reconnaissance mission over this region, met very heavy flak and had to turn back, the observer being seriously wounded and the air gunner killed.

Airborne troops and assault gliders had taken by surprise the two bridges of Vroenhoven and Veldwezelt and the allied command had at

once ordered the destruction of these for they were of vital importance to the German advance. Belgian and RAF Fairey Battles had already made almost suicidal attacks and now came the turn of the assault bomber group GBAI/54 from La Ferté-Gaucher, equipped with brand new Breguet 693 twin-engined bombers. In three sections of three aircraft each, the CO, Commandant Plou, piloting aircraft s/n 14, they plunged towards their target. The Breguet s/n 49 already had one engine on fire when it started its bombing run. Bombs were exploding amongst the enemy motorized column, but Lt Delattre, notwithstanding the state of his plane, decided to attack once again. Completely out of control during its second pass, his aircraft crashed on a group of German half-tracks. Lt Gady's aircraft, s/n 21, managed to escape along the canal banks. As for the third aircraft, s/n 10, it crash-landed on a nearby meadow. As for the aircraft who bore the serials 7, 9 and 4, they all were shot down by nearby flak whilst the CO's plane crashed out of control and exploded on impact. Breguet s/n 19, piloted by Lt Leleu, had its fuel tanks punctured and, trailing smoke, wings ablaze, it fell not far from its target although not before the crew had managed to escape by parachute. Lt Blondet, pilot of Breguet s/n 22, managed to escape after successfully dropping his bombs on parked motor transport. Thus ended this day's most important bombing operation as far as the Armée de l'Air was concerned. The RAF then took over and received the same sort of reception from a flak barrage never seen before. They behaved with the same gallantry as the French but the bridges remained in position.

Fate would have it that, apart from the already extremely embarrassing problem of the bridges over the Albert Kanaal, French reconnaissance aircraft were to discover an even more disastrous event on that fateful May 12th, 1940.

During the night of May 11th to 12th a Potez reconnaissance aircraft of the GRII/33 had taken off on a routine mission from the Athies sous Laon airfield (near Monceau le Waast where the Group headquarters was based). It had soon discovered that in the Ardennes region of Belgium, all the roads south of the river Meuse were crowded with German motor vehicles, driving at night on full headlights. The next morning, the 9th Army requested further information and a mission was flown by WO (Adjudant) Favret, with an army observer, Lt Chéry and Sgt Escane as air gunner. The Potez 63-11 s/n 48 had for a mission a low level flight in the Rochefort-Marche-Givet region of Belgium. Approaching the small town of Marche, they discovered roughly 2km west of it, the spearhead of what proved to be German panzer divisions. Headed by Henschel Hs-126 observation aircraft, motor-cycles and light armoured cars the Germans seemed to be using every available road and field in their move towards the French border. Flying at a height of only about 20m, the aircraft attacked some enemy troops with its MGs near Marche but sustained several hits from German groundfire.

Back at base after a flight of 1hr 40min, the observer had the utmost difficulty in convincing the 9th Army HQ of the seriousness of the situation. Although Lt Chéry was an officer of the armoured corps, and thus knew very well the difference between French and German tanks, the general commanding the 9th Army apparently did not believe him. This mission was not the only one to inform HQ of the disaster ahead, for at 09.30hr, another Potez 63-11 belonging to GRII/22 and flown by Captain Fouché with Lt Saint-Genis as observer and Sgt Taieb as air gunner had taken off from Chatel-Chehery for a similar reconnaissance on behalf of the 2nd Army. They discovered German motor transport, etc, crossing the river Semois at Bouillon in Belgium. What this crossing meant is only too well known today but then, notwithstanding the evidence of several very well-trained aircrew, camera film and eye witnesses, their observations were not considered seriously enough by the army command, until it was too late. The result was the break-through of the German army (12. Armee) at Sedan under List and the crossing of the river Meuse at Montherme and Sedan by units of the Panzergruppe von Kleist.

Contrary to what was going on at army headquarters, staff officers of the Armée de l'Air probably understood much better what was at stake, an and impossible effort was made to halt the Wehrmacht by means of bombing attacks. Thus on May 14th, 1940 eight available Léo 451 bombers of the Groupement de Bombardement No 6 attacked German motorized columns near Sedan, using low level tactics for which this type of bomber had not been designed. As usual, German flak had been extremely dense and one Léo 451 was shot down, many of the others bearing traces of gunfire. They were surprised on the way back when they encountered a formation of elderly Amiot 143 bombers on the way to the same target. This operation had been planned with an adequate fighter escort in mind. However, due to fierce Luftwaffe opposition, most of the fighters made available for the operation had to fight it out with Me-109s and thus some of the Amiot 143s belonging to the GBI/38 (six aircraft) and headed by the CO of the Groupement de Bombardement 10 turned back, having missed their rendezvous with their fighter escort. As for the remaining 13 bombers, drawn from GBII/38, I/34 and II/34, they went on towards their target. Taking off from their base at Roye-Amy, one of the Amiot 143s was halted by the group's CO, Commandant de Laubier, who ordered a young sergeant, named Oeillard, to get out, and took his place in the aircraft, judging it his duty to go with his formation on this, a suicide mission. Having gone into the air around noon, the formation reached their target at 13.00hr. Notwithstanding heavy flak and the sudden appearance of Me-109s, the aircraft maintained formation and dropped their bombs. Four of them were shot down, including the one with Commandant de Laubier on board, who, as second pilot, had stayed with his machine, s/n 56, till the end.

According to later German testimony, these bomber crews had performed their duty with gallantry and accuracy, the German losses being rather high and the bridges destroyed. As for the fighter pilots who had escorted them, drawn from GCIII/7 (Morane 406s), GCI/3 (Dewoitine 520s) and GCI/8 (Bloch 152s), these had been so quickly intercepted by German fighters that they had to fight it out for themselves. It was probably thanks to their acceptance of battle that not all the 180km/h Amiot 143s were shot out of the sky. As a matter of fact, GCI/3 flying the then most modern French fighter, the Dewoitine D.520, had only arrived two days before at Wez-Thuisy. Since the end of January 1940, GCI/3 had been grádually re-equipping with the type at the Cannes-Mandelieu air base on the French Riviera. Lots of teething troubles had

Of the many aircraft impressed in service with the newly-formed transport units was this sleek Bloch 160 four-engined transport plane. It bore a mixture of military roundels and civil registration letters, the latter along the fuselage, underlined with a tricoloured band.

been experienced during their conversion to this particular type, amongst others the reheating system of the wing-mounted machine guns. The CO of the group, Commandant Thibaudet, promptly decided to suppress the whole thing on arrival at the war base of Wez-Thuisy and although this took the better part of a day, the unit flew its first combat mission on May 13th, destroying amongst others, one He-111. As for the mission flown on May 14th, it certainly helped to attract several Me-109s who otherwise would have made easy meat out of the slow and cumbersome Amiot 143s. At least two Me-109s, three Me-110s and a couple of Do-17s fell to the Dewoitine's guns that day. Only one of GCI/3's fighters had been lost in the operation.

As for the total losses incurred since the 10th of the month by the Armée de l'Air, these amounted to 135 fighters, mostly Morane 406s, but also including 24 Curtiss Hawks and several Bloch 152s. Bomber losses amounted to 21, including the seven Breguet 693s on the disastrous operation over the Albert Kanaal in Belgium, ten Amiot 143s and four of the Léo 451 type.

Reconnaissance and observation aircraft counted for 76, including three of the splendid and still rare Bloch 174, and of course a large number of Potez 63-11, the type of aircraft which had borne the brunt of almost every type of recce mission before and since May 10th, 1940.

The day of May 15th spelt disaster for the whole of the French armies; on one side, the 7th Army in Belgium withdrew on the eastern bank of the river Schelde and the 'fortress' Antwerpen, whilst on the other side of the front the 9th Army practically ceased to exist, German armoured units converging towards Montcornet and Reims. Early in the morning, General Corap, who commanded the 9th Army, had phoned to the commander/air of the ZOAN, General d'Astier de la Vigerie, requesting every available air support to stop the German advance.

The situation was such that the French requested the assistance of RAF bombers, who despatched Blenheims in the Dinant region of Belgium in the late morning. Of some 270 fighters available, including those specified for the defence of the Paris region, the Armée de l'Air sent at least 150 in protection of the retreating 9th and 11th Armies. As for the bomber aircraft available that day in this ZOAN, they amounted to exactly 38. In the early evening Breguet 693 and Léo 451 bombers protected by Morane 406 and Bloch 152 fighters attempted again to halt the German advance, but in vain, as too many Wehrmacht units had already crossed the river Meuse. Considering the seriousness of the situation, one can only guess why so few bombers were drawn into these operations and here again it appears that something was decidedly wrong with what one would call the maintenance and supply organization. It is now well known that, amongst others, 222 Léo 451 bombers had been taken on strength. Roughly 50 of the modern Amiot 351/354 bombers were also taken on charge at that date, together with over 130 Glenn Martin 167s, at least 30 Douglas DB7s (Bostons) and almost 150 Breguet assault bombers of the Br 691/693 and 695 variety. Unfortunately these rather optimistic figures included a great number of bombers that were either at maintenance units awaiting vital parts of their equipment to get them operational, or on the other hand, bomber units still busy with operational conversion to a particular type.

Amongst such units on May 17th was the GBII/34 stationed at Nangis and partially re-equipped with Amiot 354 bombers. Very modern for its day, powered by two Gnome et Rhône engines of 2,500hp each, having a bomb load of two tons and a cruising speed of 400km/h its low wing loading gave it excellent take-off characteristics at full bomb load. Easy to fly, its only shortcoming at that period was the lack of a remotely controlled 20mm rear gun. The groundcrew of GBII/34 solved the problem partially by mounting some light MGs in its place. Colonel Dagnaux, CO of this bombing group, decided to join the crew of one such Amiot 354 on a night sortie on the same date. Replacing the upper air gunner, he wanted to see for himself a bombing tactic he had preconceived, and which could be considered a forerunner of the RAF pathfinder method.

Unfortunately, the aircraft came under AA fire near the town of Guise, and only the pilot and the wireless operator were able to escape the blazing furnace the bomber had become. This same day saw the appearance of 18 Potez 631s belonging to the night fighter squadrons destined to protect the capital and who were used on strafing missions at the request of the commanding general of the 9th Army. Such was the desperate need for close support. Not suited for this particular job, two were shot down by flak, whilst another four sustained heavy damage. Incidentally, these Potez 631s belonging to the escadrilles de chasse de nuit ECN I/13, II/13, III/13 and IV/13 had frequently been mistaken for German Me-110s. The result was that already on May 13th one such Potez flown by Captain Escudier was attacked by RAF Hurricanes. On May 14th the same thing happened to another Potez 631 with fatal results. On the Belgian front May 16th and 17th had sounded a partial retreat. Curtiss Hawks of GCI/4 and Bloch 152s of the Calais stationed GC2/8 had protected French troops withdrawing near the Mechelen region whilst escorts were flown for French navy dive bombers attacking the sluice-gates at the island of Walcheren, and targets near the Schelde estuary. Of the seven fighter groups operating in support of the 7th Army only these two retained a sufficient number of aircraft capable of continuing operations. Due to a surprise attack by Dornier Do-17s at the Maubeuge airfield, temporary home of GC2/6, almost all of the 18 available Morane 406s of this unit were wiped out. Only two planes were capable of escaping to Beauvais after the attack. It would take this unit until June 4th to re-equip completely with new Bloch 152s at Chateauroux. Out of 17 Morane 406s of the GC3/3 seven were ready for action by the end of the day. They were the remnants of the previously Belgian based escadrille at Moerbeeke-Waas and the other group's squadron from Maubeuge.

On May 20th the GCII/1 was based at Buc, ie, the third squadron of this group had the honour of escorting General Weygand, Commander-in-Chief of the French army, on an inspection of the front line. Eight Bloch 152s drawn from the group, and lead by Captain Veniel, flew as escort to an Amiot 354 bomber. Taking off from the aerodrome of Le Bourget at 09.00hr they first flew to the air base of Norrent-Fontes for refuelling. Although a recce unit should have been there, the airfield was found abandoned and the general was lucky enough to find a car to continue a local inspection. Abbeville and Cambrai were at that time already in German hands and after an hour the Amiot 354 and its escort set course for Saint-Inglevert, leaving one fighter behind whose undercarriage had been destroyed on landing. At around 13.00hr the whole formation flew back to base, the CO having taken to another aircraft, his own Bloch having an unserviceable starter. It was a good thing the Amiot bomber could carry passengers . . .

Pictured prior to a routine mission are pilots of GC II/1 on Bloch 152 fighters belonging to the Groupement 21 in charge of defending the Paris and lower Seine region. A very sturdy aircraft, its armament of two HS 404 canons and two MAC 34 machine guns gave it a superior fire-power to the Curtiss Hawks for example. It could also out-turn a Dewoitine D.520.

That same day a Potez 63-11 of GAO 3/551 from Romilly-sur-Seine had a strange adventure.

Taking off at dawn for a routine recce mission near Laon, aircraft No 365 piloted by Staff Sgt (sergeant-chef) Courmes suddenly met a Ju-52 transport at roughly 1,500m slightly underneath him. Going in for the attack and closing to a range of 20m, the pilot decided to go under the German to avoid a collision. On breaking to starboard his left wingtip suddenly touched the Ju-52, who had probably started his descent at the same moment, trying to escape the next pass of the Potez 63-11. Losing height, the French pilot managed to recover and bring his aircraft home safely. As for the German transport, it crash-landed and was later identified by another Potez of the same unit.

Notwithstanding the retreating front, some groups received the equipment they had been waiting for for so long. Thus the Glenn Martin 167-equipped GBI/62 and I/63, who had arrived from North Africa recently, received at long last part of their bomb release equipment which had been stored at an MU at Nanterre. This was not the only thing they required to be operational, as apparently very few of them had armoured protection for their crews, defensive armament had not been checked carefully, etc. Every effort was made by their gallant ground crews to get them into the air with a chance of matching the enemy and they joined the other Glenn Martin 167-equipped units GBII/62 and II/63 to form the nucleus of the Groupement de Bombardement No 1. Two other bomber groups, GBI/19 and II/19, equipped with recently arrived Douglas DB7s completed this Groupement. So big was the shortage of available recce aircraft that on May 24th four of these Douglas DB7s were detached to Orly, near Paris, to serve as strategic reconnaissance for the first air division. In fact they flew only one mission in the Valenciennes region before joining their parent unit at Evreux once more.

Stationed previously at Avignon, both GBI/21 and GBII/21 should have been recipients of Amiot 354 bombers. Unfortunately, only a handful of them were delivered to these units and when ordered to the front line in the ZOAN they still had a certain number of elderly Bloch 210s on charge. The original six Amiot 354s had been supplemented by four others, albeit unarmed, and on May 26th two of the twin fin and rudder version of this bomber, designated Amiot 351, joined the GBI/21 at La Ferté-Gaucher. Thus both these bombing groups operated with a modern bomber, at least the equivalent of what the other side could offer, and at the same time an elderly contraption, just good enough for training purposes.

On the night of May 22nd to 23rd different bombing sorties were flown near towns such as Doullens, Mézières, etc, which had been evacuated by the French army. Their aim was to bomb these towns so as to block the main thoroughfares. Long range reconnaissance missions were flown towards this author's birthplace, Gent, on the Brussels-Gent, and also on the Brussels-Namur line. As for the recce units, several of these, belonging originally to the ZOAE and ZOAS operational regions, had been transferred to the ZOAN, amongst them GAO546, 543, etc. All flew the Potez 63-11s and were mostly operated for missions in the Somme region and the Aisne. Wherever possible the high command, or for that matter regional commands, tried to concentrate what air support there was available. Thus on May 23rd the available Potez 63-11s of GAO515 arrived at Château-Thierry whilst a sister unit GAO510, also with Potez 63-11s, took up station at Mantes-Gassicourt. Several Groupes de Chasse (fighter groups) had also been taken from other operational zones to augment the potential of the ZOAN.

One such, the GCIII/6 flying Morane 406 fighters, had left its base in the Jura region to start operations at Coulommiers. Typical of the unpreparedness of some wartime airfields, was the fact that this unit found the base squadron stationed there in a state of complete apathy towards them. Nothing seemed ready; there was no ammunition and no petrol, not even oxygen bottles. As for the RAF Blenheim squadron stationed on the other side of the field, this was lucky enough to have its own ground support. It nevertheless enabled the French to get their complete unit airborne the next day, and 18 Moranes started a sweep in the Cambrai-Le Catelet region in the late afternoon. Having had a skirmish with a mixed formation of Me-109s and Me-110s it lost three pilots and six aircraft. On May 24th the remaining Moranes of this GCIII/6 were to fly as escort on one of the first operational sorties by French Glenn Martin 167 bombers. The mission had to be flown in the Cambrai-Arras region and due to the large amount of cloud, the top cover provided by Dewoitine D.520 fighters of GCII/3 remained unseen. Attacking a formation of German bombers, they were in turn attacked by the usual Me-109 formation, losing their CO, Commandant Castanier, during the fight.

The Cambrai-Arras-Amiens region certainly seemed to focus the attention of both Armée de l'Air and Luftwaffe alike and the French apparently did all what was possible to stop the German advance with the few means of retaliation available to them. The assault bombers of GBAI/51 and II/51 attacked this region with everything they could muster. These included not only the modern Breguet 693s but also Potez 633s, a bomber/attack development of the original P.631.

Already on May 20th 14 aircraft drawn from the assault bomber units had attacked German troop concentrations. One of the Potez 633s had been shot down by light flak, whilst another, s/n 36, had crashed on landing. On May 22nd GBAII/51 could still muster nine P.633s, incidentally all were aircraft which had once been destined for foreign air forces, but had been withheld by the French government on the outbreak of war. These aircraft were no match against either the Luftwaffe or the light flak concentrations the Wehrmacht could put up with some of its armoured and motorized columns. Another unit, GBAII/35 still had some on strength on May 26th but at the end of the month that type of aircraft received interdiction to fly on front line missions.

It should be noted that from the onset of 1940 the P.633 had been destined as an operational training aircraft for the future Breguet 691/693 crews, 60 to 80 flying hours being required on the former before conversion to the Breguets. If Potez's twin-engined fighter had the distinction of serving albeit in different versions, in practically every conceivable role for the Armée de l'Air, it had also the dubious honour of resembling a bit too closely another twin-engined conception from over the Rhine, the Me-110. In the early evening of May 20th a section (patrouille simple) of three Potez 631s led by Lt Guiller was suddenly attacked by six Dewoitine 520 fighters. One of the aircraft of the ECN

2/13 (night fighter squadron) was severely mauled by the Dewoitines before the latter realized their mistake. The next day, at roughly 15km south-west of the town of Senlis, a newly arrived fighter unit, GCII/3, equipped with Dewoitine 520s was keen to fight it out with the Luftwaffe. Since its arrival the previous day at the little aerodrome of Betz-Bouillancy it had looked for an opportunity to meet the enemy, who indeed showed up on May 21st in the form of a large formation of Heinkel He-111 bombers. The result was disastrous indeed for the Germans, no fewer than eight of their bombers being shot down. One can easily imagine the state of mind of the pilots of GCII/3, when flying back to base they suddenly encountered a slim fighter with a twin fin and rudder. One of them, flown by a young lieutenant, attacked the 'enemy' from astern, scoring a few hits on the tailplane. Unfortunately, this 'enemy' was none other than a Potez 631 flown by Adjudant (Warrant Officer) Martin with Adjudant Guichard as air gunner. Both belonged to ECN4/13, one of the original night fighter squadrons destined to protect the capital, but also used for other duties, due to the circumstances then prevailing. Martin kept his heading, having recognized the Dewoitine himself and hoping his opponent would have done the same. Unfortunately this apparently was not the case and only by vigorous evasive action did he manage to escape the second pass. After the fourth pass, the crew of the Potez had doubts about the D.520 pilots' nationality. It could have been a captured aircraft after all . . .

When the latter made its fifth pass, and missed again, Adjudant Guichard opened fire at last, with fatal results for the Dewoitine pilot, his fighter crashing north of Senlis. A couple of days later a Potez 631 of another night fighter squadron, ECN I/13, experienced a similar incident, this time by Bloch 152s. Still another Potez, flown by Sgt-Chef Collinot, had the same fate. Badly wounded, he managed to crash-land his aircraft. Obviously this state of affairs could not go on, so the air staff decided to apply some particular means of identification for these ill-fated Potez 631s. Fuselage roundels were surrounded by a white circle, and a four-metre white band was painted along the fuselage, on both sides of the roundel. In addition, most fighter airfields received a visit from a Potez 631, to help everybody identify the machine. Meantime the war was going on, and on May 22nd Intelligence captured a German message from the Cambrai region again requesting Stuka support for the Arras region.

No less than 18 Dewoitine 520s, again of GC II/3 patrolled the Bapaume-Cambrai sector in support of counter-attacking French armoured units.

Arriving around 17.10hr over their target, a large formation of Ju-87 Stukas, the French started their attack at the moment where the Stukas split formation to start their dive bombing. Twelve D.520s went after them, while six others gave top cover. In a few minutes, not less than 11 Stukas had been shot down. In the meantime ten or so Me-109s tried to intervene, but only one D.520 was shot down, its pilot escaping by parachute. On the way back some Dewoitines ran out of fuel, and the leader of the formation, Commandant Morlat, had to land at Villacoublay, whilst another pilot crash-landed 3km from base within sight of the runway at Betz. The following incident befell Flight Sergeant Tourné of the same unit.

Interesting air shot of Potez 63-11, the aircraft nearest to the camera sporting the white fuselage band, and fuselage roundel surrounded in white, introduced since the regrettable incidents of May 21st. The second aircraft of the formation still sports the normal paint scheme and was thus more liable to be taken for a Me-110.

Short of fuel, Sergeant-Chef Tourné landed his aircraft at the airfield of Poix which, shortly before, had been abandoned by the RAF. Aided by some local inhabitants and with the help of a car left by the British, he managed to re-join the French lines. At the HQ of Grandvilliers he received a voucher enabling him to buy 200 litres of fuel at Beauvais. Back at base in the very early morning of the next day and escorted by an army armoured car and a truckload of soldiers, he refuelled his aircraft and took off at the very moment German troops entered the village. On the way to his home base he was jumped by three Me-109s and escaped only thanks to cloud cover. He was then lucky enough to join a formation of Bloch 152s from another unit and landed at their base of Chantilly, where he rearmed and joined his own unit again within twenty-four hours.

If, as has been told, the regular units had had their share of sorrow and glory so far, another sort of Armée de l'Air formation, the Escadrilles Légères de Défense or Escadrilles de Chasse de Défense (ELD or ECD) have to be mentioned as well.

These escadrilles, in strength more equivalent to an RAF flight than a squadron, were composed mostly of pilots belonging to the reserve, or of those pilots and aircraft engaged in special units, flying and gunnery schools, etc. In addition, part of this number consisted of test pilots attached to the aircraft factories and who were to form local defence flights.

Although it is generally accepted that the official instruction from the Armée de l'Air headquarters, pertaining to the formation of these auxiliary units, came on May 11th, there were in fact some such local defence flights in existence before that date.

Such was the case of the Chateaudun base, the big MU and aircraft storage depot of the air force. This station had formed a four-aircraft 'patrouille de défense' since March 1940, equipped with Bloch 152s. Although the ferry pilots of this flight had little experience of fighter operations, one of them nevertheless managed to down an He-111 on May 12th.

The day before, other ELD (local defence flights) were formed all around France to protect the various aircraft plants. Thus were established Toulouse-Blagnac Bourges, Nantes-Bougaenais, etc. The aircraft were taken either straight from the production line, or from those that were there for repair of overhaul. As related above, pilots were mostly the aircraft company's own test pilots, or Armée de l'Air pilots from nearby fighter OTUs, reservists, etc. Orders were also given for the protection of the various airbases all over the country. In the case of advanced flying schools, OTUs and the like, there was of course no problem in finding adequately trained pilots. As for their mounts, this was a different question, and depended as to what was available at each particular airbase.

Due to circumstances then prevailing, most records about these units were lost, although others had more luck. At the end of the war, their victories could be numbered at 20, of which nine were confirmed. With little more than four to six aircraft available per unit, with the usual rate of unserviceability or aircraft under maintenance as for every unit anywhere in the world, this was no mean feat. It must not be forgotten that all these defence flights depended for their ammunition and spares

Relegated to second line duties due to their inferior performance, many of the Bloch 151 fighters served with training establishments and secondary and local defence formations such as the ECD 1/55 from Tours. Pictured here are factory fresh aircraft.

supply on what the regional command, or nearby aircraft maintenance units, could offer them. As for the operational aspect, missions were mostly flown after a local alert was given. Enemy contact was also sometimes made by sheer chance whilst on a local patrol. Of all these units, the 'Escadrilles de Chasse de Défense' from Tours and Bourges were perhaps the biggest and the Tours unit, known as ECDI/55 finished the war as a Groupe de Chasse I/55. At the aircraft depots and MUs of Romorantin at Avord, Montpellier, Chartres, Etampes, Orleans-Bricy and at the Ecole de l'Air at Salon, everywhere possible such defence flights were established. Their main equipment was the Bloch 151 fighter. This unlucky predecessor of the Bloch 152 family had not been accepted for operational use, and had been relegated to various CIC (Centres d'Instructions de la Chasse). Other aircraft operated by ECD or ELD were Morane 406s or even elderly Dewoitine 501s or 510s, once the Armée de l'Air's first monoplane fighter of relatively modern design (see volume one). Elderly contraptions, at least 60 of the D-500s, were still on strength on May 10th, 1940, albeit in various states, ranging from the completely unserviceable aircraft, to one in good condition. The same applied to over 100 D-501s and some D-510s.

A lesser-known aircraft that also served these local fighter units was the Dutch-built Koolhoven FK-58A. Fourteen of these aircraft had been parked at the EAA301 (air force depot 301) at Romorantin. At least four of these went to the fighter training unit at Lyon-Bron, a unit which was mostly converting ex-Polish air arm personnel to French aeroplanes and procedures. On May 16th the Ecole de l'Air at Salon, which incidentally was one of the few units to have a local defence flight equipped with brand new Dewoitine D-520s, received orders to form a Polish-manned unit with seven of these Koolhoven FK-58As on strength. Apparently it got nine aircraft in total, some coming from

Shown here is a single fin and rudder version of the Amiot bomber known as the Type 354. This picture shows an early example with protruding bomb aimer's nose. Thirteen such bombers were on strength on May 10th, 1940, of which ten were serviceable, but unarmed . . . At the end of hostilities in June they equipped partially the GB I/21, II/21, I/34 and II/34 which also had some of the twin fin and rudder Amiot 351 on strength. Out of 66 taken on charge by the Armee de l'Air, 30 were delivered to operational units during the period May 10th to June 10th, 1940.

Etampes and others from Villacoublay. Later on, some of these Koolhovens were traced back to places such as Aulnat (four) of which two came directly from the stock at the EAA301, from Romorantin, or Caen-Carpiquet. All flown by Polish pilots, little is known of their operational career. On the other hand, the Bourges formed factory flight was equipped straight away with brand new Curtiss Hawk H-75As coming off the production line. Ten were in service under Commandant Haegelen, a World War I ace. Several victories were confirmed, one on June 6th by the CO himself. Around that period a flight of four Bloch 151s manned by Polish pilots under Lt Laprowski joined the Bourges ELD.

As for the Tours-based ECDI/55 mentioned earlier, this mustered at least nine Bloch 151s and one Potez 630 twin-engined fighter. This was used mostly for giving cover or recce flights. Headed by Captain Clavel with Commandant Smits as the organiser, this little squadron had also at least one Polish pilot amongst its ranks, as well as a Sergeant-Chef Verrier, who was to become better known at a later period at an operational theatre.

Whilst these small auxiliary units had been trying to cut their teeth in anger, the other Armée de l'Air formations had certainly no problems in doing so, with an ever retreating front and a particularly aggressive Luftwaffe.

Wherever possible, bombers had been sent out to try to halt the German advance. This was to no avail, especially as the tactics used were completely wrong, and exactly the opposite as to what would be done by the Allies later on. Each mission was flown by very small numbers of aircraft and thus the bomber force, or what remained of it, was destroyed piecemeal. In the morning of May 24th German bombers

attacked again the aerodrome of La Ferté-Gaucher where GBI/21 and II/21 were stationed. One of the few Amiot 354 bombers there was destroyed, whilst another was damaged. A couple of elderly Bloch 210s were also written off. That evening a night op was prepared for three Bloch 210s on the Cambrai-Douai road, but the flak got one down with fatal results for the crew. May 25th was again a bad day, as several Bloch 210s had to turn back from a mission against German motor transport in the Saint-Quentin region due to bad weather. One of them even crashed on take-off; the same thing happening two days later. On the 25th an Amiot 354, s/n 37, had been lost whilst crash-landing, and on the 28th during an attack on the Luftwaffe occupied aerodrome of Cambrai-Niergnies by six aircraft, one of the Amiot 354s was destroyed on landing. On May 29th it was the turn of an Amiot 351 to be written off, having lost a wheel during the final landing run. At the end of the month the Groupement de Bombardement 6 had planned a large raid in the Amiens-Abbeville region. Seventeen Léo 451s took part in this raid, but again losses were high as eight bombers failed to return.

In the meantime, another part of history was being written between May 26th and June 3rd, with the evacuation of Dunkirk (Dunkerque) by the British Expeditionary Force, and part of the French army which had been encircled in that region. As far as air support for that battle was concerned, this had been mostly a matter for the RAF although some Armée de l'Air units intervened from the other side of the Channel, operating from Lympne. These comprised Bloch 152s from GCII/8 who, as a unit in support of the French navy, had been ordered by Admiral North to move to Britain when its base at Mardyck was too close to German lines. Also at Lympne were a number of Potez 63-11s of GRI/14 and two Glenn Martin 167s from GB I/63. The 13 Bloch 152s had left France in the early afternoon of May 30th and were intended to operate in protection of the encircled 1st French Army, which was retreating from Lille towards the coast and Dunkirk. Although there was plenty of petrol available for the French aircraft, these couldn't use the engine oil available there, made for Hurricanes and not for the Bloch 152, which needed another specification. A French transport aircraft of the Bloch 220 type arrived only 24 hours later, so on May 31st only one of the Potez 63-11s took off for a reconnaissance mission on behalf of the French army, hard pressed by Guderian's panzers, since the surrender of the Belgian army on May 28th. This Potez of GRI/14 was thus escorted by RAF Hurricanes. On June 1st, however, eight Bloch 152s and Hurricanes took off at 14.30hr, again as escorts for a Potez 63-11. The latter was to direct French artillery towards German batteries near the 'Camp des Dunes' where French soldiers were waiting to embark. The French arrived over Dunkirk whilst the Luftwaffe was starting a bombing attack over the port. A Ju-88 fell to the guns of two NCO pilots, Adjudant Nicolle being responsible for another German, this time an He-111, who crash-landed on the beach with one engine out. Although they were almost attacked by a formation of Hurricanes, and received also a warm welcome from French ack-ack batteries, the whole formation managed to cross the Channel again. With the withdrawal of Dunkirk at an end, both GRI/14 and GCII/8 regained France.

During these last days of May, there had been heavy fighting in the Somme region and both the reconnaissance and bomber units of the

Armée de l'Air had been in action wherever possible. Losses had been high too, as up to May 25th the bombing arm had lost 112 aircraft, 50 on operations, 36 due to enemy bombing and the remainder due to other causes. Of these, Groupement de Bombardement No 6 lost 16 Léo 451s on operations against the enemy and 25 aircraft of the same type for other reasons, accidents and enemy bombing included. This state of affairs had been so serious that all the GB (Groupe de Bombardement) belonging to this Groupement and who had been equipped with Léo 451s, were withdrawn from front line operations on May 21st. Forty new Léo 451s were acquired at various airfields in the rear, such as Bordeaux, Bougenais and Ambérieu. On the other hand, the air force depot EAA301 had delivered the following types of new aircraft between the period May 10th and 28th: 18 Amiot 351/354s, 39 Breguet 693 attack bombers, 23 Douglas DB7s, 14 Glenn Martin 167s and 64 Léo 451s. Even the obsolete Amiot 143s and Bloch 210s which could be spared from other units at the rear went on operations again. On May 31st, day bombers made sorties *en force*. German convoys to the north of Abbeville were attacked by 18 Glenn Martin 167s at dawn, one of them managed even to shoot down an Me-109. Later on, 12 Douglas DB7s undertook a low-level sortie in the Saint-Quentin and Peronne regions. They had less luck than the Glenns, as three of them were shot down for the loss of one Me-109. In the mid-afternoon it was the turn of Breguet 693s of GBA18, who went after German armour south-west of the town of Abbeville. One Breguet was lost in this operation and at the end of the same afternoon, 21 of the Groupement de Bombardement's Léo 451s that had returned to the front, went on missions in the same region bombing German panzers and motor transport. With no fighter protection at all, they were intercepted by the usual large formation of Me-109s and lost 8 of theirs for two Germans downed. GRI/14 and I/35 got 13 Potez6 3-11s between them, these aircraft having belonged to GRII/52 who left Roquencourt for Bordeaux-Mérignac to re-equip with Bloch 174s. GRI/36 also in Potez 63-11s left its base of the ZOAE region and took up station at Le Havre. If these 'Groupes de Reconnaissance' or GR had been more or less receiving replacement aircraft, their colleagues of the 'Groupes Aériens d'Observation' or GAO had been less lucky. Since May 10th they had in fact lost 114 aircraft in combat or due to enemy attacks, etc, whereas the GR units had only lost 80. It was thus intended to re-equip 12 of the GAO with six Potez 63-11s each, and on May 28th 30 of these planes were at the disposal of the armies in the field.

At the start of June, the Luftwaffe High Command had inaugurated a series of bombing attacks on the larger of the French cities, such as Marseille on June 1st and Lyon on the 2nd. It was during the attack of June 3rd that a new unit first saw action. This differed somewhat from the other AA units, insofar as it was manned practically exclusively with Polish personnel, and that it flew the Caudron CR.714 'Cyclone' light-weight fighter. This unit, known as GCI/145, had originated at Lyon-Bron on March 1st, 1940 as part of the Polish fighter school (ECI) or Ecole de Chasse et d'Instruction. Eight of the 47 Cyclone fighters on the strength of the Armée de l'Air had been taken on charge by the Polish pilots at that date. In fact they had to take these at Villacoublay, where they were training till May 27th/29th.

On May 31st, 1940 two bombing units, GB I/19 and II/19 saw operation on the DB 7 in France. They had received their new mounts piecemeal since the start of the 'Battle of France' twelve out of seventeen being serviceable on May 29th. On May 31st, 12 of these DB 7s attacked German panzers and motorised units in the Saint-Quentin-Peronne-Ham sector, losing three. The picture shows a Douglas DB 7 of the GB II/32 stationed in North Africa.

Different bugs had to be ironed out of these 'Cyclones' and there was even one fatal accident costing the life of Second Lt Dobrzinski on May 19th.

Whatever the consequences of these teething troubles might have been, it was thanks to the perseverance of both Commandant Kepinski and Commandant Lionel de Marmier (a well-known pre-war pilot, who had already been responsible for part of the organisation of the AA's transport command), that this fighter group went operational altogether. From Villacoublay it was ordered to Dreux for defence of the capital and it arrived at its new station on June 2nd. Colonel Pawlikowski was in overall command and besides 31 Polish pilots, not including the two squadron commanders, or the staff pilots, there were 125 ground crew, of which only four were of French nationality. Thirty-four Caudron Cyclones were on strength of which 18 were available for immediate action.

Thus dawned the day of June 3rd, with every possible Groupe de Chasse made available to thwart the Luftwaffe's attack on Paris. Groupement de Chasse 21 under General Pinsard, with three Groupes de Chasse (GCI/1, II/9 and II/1) of Bloch 152s and one Groupe de Chasse (GCI/6) of Morane 406s were to intercept the enemy formation before it arrived over Paris. In this it was supported by Groupement 23 under General Romatet with four Groupes de Chasse, of which one flew Dewoitine 520s, one Bloch 152s and two were equipped with Morane 406s (GCI/3, I/8, III/7 and III/1 respectively). The Groupement 22 under Colonel Dumêmes had orders to intercept the Germans on their way back, with five Groupes de Chasse (GCI/5, II/5, I/2, II/2 and II/7 respectively), flying Curtiss Hawks (two), Morane 406s (two) and the remaining one flying Dewoitine 520s. Further, there were also available the night fighter units, stationed around the capital, which were equipped with Potez 631s.

The general alert was given to all fighter units involved about 13.06hr, but being transmitted via the Eiffel Tower the message was blurred. Thus, many fighter squadrons did not even react to it. In the meantime a formation of 200 plus German bombers, flying between 4,000 and 5,000m, was converging on the capital from different directions. They had the usual close escort of Me-110s, with large formations of Me-109s as top cover.

Around 13.10hr, the Polish-manned Cyclones of GCI/145 intercepted, getting in contact with Me-109s near Etampes, where they shot down two of their opponents. About the same time a formation of 17 Dewoitine 520s from GCI/3 had taken off from Meaux and made contact near Corbeil with Dornier Do-17s flying at roughly 5,000m. In the ensuing mêlée, three Germans were hit as well as one of the attacking Me-109s, but two French fighters were also shot down. One of the patrolling Potez 631s of ECNI/13 (night fighter squadron I/13) was also jumped by several Me109s and shot down in the Lassigny region. Fourteen Bloch 152s from GCI/1 took off from Chantilly at 13.20hr, followed closely by eight aircraft of the same type belonging to GCII/9. Both these formations were practically in touch with the enemy from take-off onwards, and sustained heavy losses. Three aircraft of GCI/1 were shot down in rapid succession but one of them, piloted by Captain Maréchal, succeeded in hitting an Me-109 with fatal results for the latter, before he crashed himself in the Oise. Lt Daval of GCII/9 scored a hit on another Me-109 before crashing himself. This was his sixth victory. Another four aircraft of this unit were shot down, but Captain Canel was the only one to escape by parachute. When the Germans appeared over the aerodrome of Claye-Souilly, a patrol of Bloch 152 aircraft from GCI/8 managed to intercept them and shot down one Junkers Ju-88. With bombs scattering all over their aerodrome, aircraft from GCII/1 took off at 13.30hr and managed to down one Do-17 and one Me-109, but lost one of their Bloch 152s, two others being seriously damaged. Fate had it that this air battle for Paris would be an 'allied' event, as besides the French and Polish crews already mentioned, four Fiat Cr-42 biplane fighters of the Belgian detachment from Chartres, remnants of the 3rd and 4th squadrons of the 2nd Fighter Regiment of Nivelles, also took part in the operation. This unit, under Major Lamarche, was awaiting transfer to North Africa. The Belgians took off on alert at 13.35hr when their base was already under bombing attack, but their elderly Fiats could only intercept a Dornier Do-17 formation. Nevertheless, they managed to hit seriously two of their opponents, but it was impossible to check later if these were brought down over French lines. The formation of Morane 406s of GCIII/7 from Coulommiers had even less luck. Normally this Groupe de Chasse should have been re-equipping with Dewoitine 520s, but for reasons unknown, another unit went before them. So they had to operate their worn-out Moranes with the result that a 'patrouille triple' (three sections of three aircraft each) headed by WO (Adjudant) Littolf had the misfortune to encounter a formation of He-111s who escaped in a shallow dive. Jumped by Me-109s, they owed their safe return to base solely to a formation of Dewoitine 520s from GCI/3. On their way back from Paris, another formation of Do-17s was intercepted by 21 Curtiss Hawks from GCI/5, who had left their base at Saint-Dizier at 13.35hr.

Led by their CO, Commandant Murtin, this formation had amongst its ranks such aces as Captain Accart, Lt Marin la Meslée and others, and was considered one of the 'crack' units of the French Air Force. They intercepted the Dorniers at about 4,500m, at least 40 of them, flying in close formation on a north-easterly heading between Reims and Epernay. Over 50 Me-109s and 110s together jumped on the French formation, whilst it was attacking the Dorniers from the rear. Cdt Murtin, being attacked by an Me-110, managed to take violent evasive action, his Curtiss already hit in several places, and coming in to attack the German, shot him out of the sky after a very long burst. Notwithstanding the numerical superiority of the German fighters, the long training of these GCI/5 pilots proved worthwhile in that only one of them was killed for a total of five Germans shot down, including one bomber. It was proof too that the Germans had done their best to protect their bombers. At the end of the day, the score of this big attack on Paris could be stated as follows:

Thirteen AA airfields and three others had been attacked with the loss of six aircraft and a further seven damaged. These belonged to the fighting formations of the ZOAN. Although the motor-car plants of Citroën and Renault had been hit, they were far from put out of service. Another 13 factories were hit, but sustained only slight damage and several railway junctions around Paris had been cut off, albeit only for one day. At the aerodrome of Le Bourget five precious Amiot 351 bombers were destroyed. The same thing happened at Orly, five Dewoitine 520s being smashed under the ruins of their huge hangar.

On the other hand, the Luftwaffe sustained the loss of 26 aircraft of various types, not counting those that were damaged but managed to fly back to base. Twelve French pilots lost their lives, and also 250 civilians. In the meantime the OKW (Oberkommando der Wehrmacht) was preparing its second big offensive to try to finish off the French army, and as usual, it could count on the might of the Luftwaffe. What was the situation of the Armée de l'Air on the eve of the battle of the Aisne?

By far the greatest recipient of bomber groups was the northern zone of operations or ZOAN, who mustered not less than 17, including five assault bomber groups equipped with Breguet 693s and some Breguet 691s. Other groups had Glenn Martin 167s, Douglas DB7s, Léo 451s and Amiots of the 351/354 variety on strength, together with obsolete Bloch 210s and Amiot 143s for good measure.

In general, the five Groupements de Bombardement to which these groups belonged could muster modern material as only Groupement No 9 had groups of mixed composition. These were GBI/21, II/21 I/34 and II/34, who were the recipients of 25 of the modern Amiot 351/354s and of not less than 35 Amiot 143s and 17 Bloch 210s. The other units had a grand total of some 46 Glenn Martin 167s, 17 Douglas DB7s, and 28 Léo 451s, together with 67 Breguet 691/693s (eight being Br.691s).

Unfortunately, not all these bombers were available for immediate action that day, and in fact only half of them were available for rapid deployment. Fighters of the ZOAN were deployed in three Groupe-

One of the most promising designs as far as bombers were concerned, was certainly the Amiot 351-354 series. Illustrated here is the twin fin and rudder type 351, bearing the serial number X-180.

ments of which one, the 'Groupement de Chasse de Nuit' or night fighter group, comprised 38 Potez 631s of which 15 were available for immediate operation.

As for the Groupements 21 and 23, these mustered 82 and 202 fighters respectively, of which not less than 210 were available. If compared to the bombers, the ground crews of these fighter units had certainly to be congratulated. The Polish-manned Caudron Cyclones were not included in this total, although some of these remained on operations at least till June 13th. Long range reconnaissance units could muster 74 aircraft, of which 40 were ready for immediate use. These included 13 of the Bloch 174 type, of which only six were in a state of immediate readiness. The remaining aircraft belonged to the Potez family of twin-engined aircraft (P.630-637 and 63-11). All these aircraft belonged to the GRII/33, I/35 I/36, I/44 and II/55.

Short range reconnaissance units of the GAO type amounted to 12, with 72 aircraft available, of which 48 were at immediate readiness, and included only 39 Potez 63-11s as modern aeroplanes.

The eastern zone of operations comprised three Groupements de Bombardement with a total of eight Groupes de Bombardement. On the evening of June 5th 44 out of a total of 107 bombers were ready for action. These comprised seven out of 21 four-engined Farman F.222/223 bombers, 21 Léo 451s out of 58 and 16 Amiot 143s out of 28. One wonders what these latter still could do even during night operations. Fighters were again better off, as their two Groupements (Nos 22 and 24) could muster a total of 192 planes, 157 of which were ready to enter action at once. Groupement 24 was the smaller of the two and had in fact only two fighter groups, namely GCII/2 still with Morane 406s and GCII/7 with Dewoitine 520s. It speaks highly for this latter group that out of 29 aircraft on strength, not less than 27 were available for immediate operations. Groupement 22 had no less than five Groupes de Chasse under its command, three of them with Curtiss Hawks, one with Bloch 152s and one with Morane 406s. This was GCI/2 at Damblain, which had 16 out of 21 planes at readiness. Short range observation, as done by the GAO, accounted for 62 Potez 63-11s, only 32 of them 'bons de guerre' as French terminology had it. The long range GR units, six of them in total, had 36 out of 53 aircraft good for immediate use, of which 26 were Potez 63-11s and three of the superior Bloch 174s.

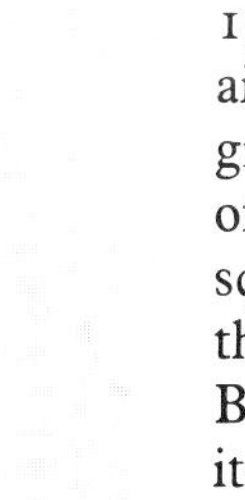

For comparison, Armée de l'Air losses on the morning of June 5th amounted to 473 fighters, 120 bombers, and 194 reconnaissance and observation aircraft. On the other hand, the fighter arm alone claimed 550 victories, 375 of which were more than confirmed. It should be noted that these claims were for the period from May 10th till June 5th, 1940 only, and that the losses stated above comprised not only those aircraft that were shot down in action but also those destroyed on the ground by bombing or by accident. As defence against the oncoming offensive, the Armée de l'Air could rely on three fighter and six bomber squadrons of the Advanced Air Striking Force of the RAF. However, these units themselves were but a shadow of what they once were. Beginning with their by now well-known tactics, the Luftwaffe started its attacks in the very early morning, around 4 o'clock. Three Panzerkorps moved to the attack across the river Somme, the 15th Panzerkorps of Hoth being lucky enough to find an intact railway bridge. The other

Close up of a war-weary Glenn Martin 167 bomber with which four groupes de bombardement were equipped during the May-June campaign. Operating with success, especially at the later stages of the campaign, it also saw action against the Italians when that country declared war on France in June 1940. Out of 231 taken on charge on June 25th, only slightly over forty were operational in France. Many were still in crates in North Africa, others dispersed at various MUs awaiting equipment, and one bomber unit, GB 1/39, was stationed in Syria.

armoured units attacked from the Amiens and Peronne bridgeheads but, contrary to what had happened on May 10th, the new C-in-C of the French army, General Weygand, had been able to form different strongholds which effectively halted the advancing German panzers and infantry. Unfortunately, on June 6th, some parts of the front gave way due to enemy pressure and other reasons outwith the scope of this book. In the evening of the 7th, Rommel's panzers were only 40km from the Seine and Rouen . . .

On June 5th the Armée de l'Air had again tried to halt the offensive power and 18 Breguet 693 attack bombers escorted by 15 Curtiss Hawks from GCI/4 had effectively mauled units of the 14th Panzerkorps near Amiens. No losses were incurred by the bombers and on the way back eight German fighters were shot down for the loss of one Curtiss. A successful operation indeed. Unfortunately, another attack of 12 Breguets near Peronne ended with the loss of five of them. In the early afternoon a formation of 18 Glenn Martin 167 bombers, again with a top cover of 23 fighters, dropped not less than 13 tons of bombs on German armour that had penetrated the Braye sur Somme area. Two of the Glenns were lost during this operation, one by flak and the other by fighters. Decidedly an all-out effort of the French bombing arm, the series continued with ops flown by 12 Douglas DB7s, again against German panzers and motorised elements. One of GBI/19's planes was lost during this mission. Around 18.00hr, ten Breguet 693s attacked in the Nesle-Ablaincourt sector of the Péronne bridgehead, whilst an hour later a formation of seven other Breguets took over, again in the Nesle-Marchelepot sector. Both these operations were flown without loss. In one day, 126 sorties had been flown by bombers alone, with at least 60 tons of bombs dropped. During the night, various operations were flown by the obsolete Bloch 210s and Amiot 143s of Groupement 9 and also of the ZOAE. Even a handful of Farman F.222/223s bombed such places as Köln, Frankfurt and Bonn in Germany. Unfortunately, this all-out effort of the French bombing force and its gallant crews, whatever its local results had been, could not stop the break-through of the French front. From June 5th till 10th, the retreating French armies obliged the Armée de l'Air to evacuate most of its bases it then had near the front. If the flying elements did this in good order as usual, the ground echelons had to cope with many different problems, ranging from constant air attacks to squirmishes with advanced parties of the Wehrmacht, etc. But before their retreat to new airfields, the fighter arm too had made June 5th its day. No less than 66 German aircraft were claimed that day for the loss of 15 fighters, those damaged not included. Ten French fighter pilots lost their lives that day. During a sortie flown by five Bloch 152s of the GCI/8, who flew escort to a Potez 63-11 of the GAO501 the following surprising incident occurred. Jumped by a formation of ten Me-109s around 10 o'clock, the latter shot down the French reconnaissance aircraft almost at once, but not before several of the escorts managed to shoot down some of the attacking Germans. One of the Bloch 152s, piloted by Sergeant-Chef Liautard, who had followed the Potez 63-11 during the latter's evasive manoeuvres, found himself suddenly under fire from three Me-109s. Diving like hell, and still with the Germans on his tail, he managed to get rid of two of them. His aircraft being heavy on the controls, he hedge-hopped along, hoping to escape the sole Messerschmitt who still clung to his tail. Each time the German was in position to shoot, the Bloch turned away, but the latter's superior speed made the French fighter increasingly difficult to hold, and this barely a few metres above the ground. His rpms falling, and the engine starting to spurt, Liautard knew the end was coming, so when the German made another pass, he opened fire with his guns at the moment the other broke away at about 10m distance. Pulling over the stick, he brought his Bloch so close to the German that his propeller blades touched the other's fuselage aft of the cockpit. This was bad luck as he had intended to ram the German's tail. His plane now completely out of control, Liautard just had time to crash-land on a meadow, which by sheer chance happened to be under him. As he was getting out, the Me-109 appeared again, tried to make another pass but, seemingly out of control, crashed a few kilometres away. Around 17.00hr that day, a mixed formation of Dewoitine 520s of both GCI/3 and II/7 were flying a sweep near the front when at 8,000m over Compiegne they were attacked by a two-formation team of 40 Me-109s. At the outset two D.520s went down in flames, but the section led by Captain Hugo of the GCII/7 turned on to the enemy and Second Lt Pomier-Layragues shot down one of the Me-109s, the German pilot escaping by parachute. He then continued towards another group of Me-109s, but in the dogfight which followed, was himself shot down, his aircraft crashing on a house at Marissel. It was a pity he never knew whom he had shot down, as it was none other than Hauptmann Werner Mölders, a Luftwaffe ace with several victories to his credit in Spain, Poland and France. The story goes that on his transfer to an interrogation centre, Mölders had made the request to be introduced to his former opponent . . . To this day his pilot's scarf is still in the trophy hall of the Ecole de l'Air at Salon.

The GCII/7, which had only arrived at Meaux that morning bringing 25 Dewoitine 520s as a precious reinforcement for the Groupement 23, had received a severe mauling that day. Who knows if one of the Polish pilots of GCII/7 killed that day had not been fighting it out with that same unit of Mölders' in Poland months before. During June 5th and the following three days, another dubious honour befell the pilots of GCI/6, II/2 and III/7. These Morane 406-equipped groupes de chass were instructed to halt German armour with guns. The fact that these aircraft were by that time certainly the least suitable of all French fighters for the interception role, and that on the other hand their armament comprised besides their two machine-guns, a 20mm gun, had been responsible for the high command's decision. Never did the number of aircraft available for these missions exceed 36. Although they certainly accounted for some local successes the wrecks of at least 12 of them between Somme and Seine were testimony of the accuracy of the German ack-ack units, and the gallantry with which these pilots went into the attack. On June 7th, the day the battle for the Somme could be considered as finished, the different GAO with their Potez 63-11s got their share of work from the various army HQ. One such, GAO501, was instructed to patrol along the Roye-Nesle, Canal du Nord sector.

The following will serve to illustrate the sort of difficulties these reconnaissance and observation units could encounter whilst performing their missions.

Orders had been given to start the mission at dawn. As bad luck would have it, the first aircraft checked had a faulty propeller which could not be put into coarse pitch, this due to a leak in the compressed air supply. The second had its starboard engine unserviceable, whilst the third showed a complete failure of the intercom. It was 06.40hr when the crew of Lt Lefebvre finally took off in the fourth machine. Having no fighter protection, the whole mission had to be flown at low level. Near the region of Champien enemy anti-aircraft fire punctured one of the fuel tanks whilst other damage was also sustained by the aircraft. However, the Potez did its job well and at 08.00hr the crew landed at Chantilly les Aigles to report to the local HQ of the air force/army coordination centre, from whence the pilot was driven to the commanding general of the 7th Army. The enemy panzers located during this mission were later attacked by Douglas DB7 bombers of the 2nd Groupement de Bombardement. On June 11th, Italy in turn declared war on France, whilst the German forces had three bridgeheads on the lower Seine the next day. On the east, the Marne was crossed at Château-Thierry whilst the Panzerkorps von Kleist crossed the Aisne at Berry au Bac. Reims fell quickly into German hands and the might of eight Panzerdivisionen succeeded in breaking through in the Champagne region. During these two days the Caudron Cyclones of GCI/145 had been in operation whenever their serviceability allowed. Cdt Kepinski claimed one Me-110 over Rouen in the afternoon of the 8th with no casualties for his outfit, except for one Cyclone which made a forced landing, riddled with 30 bullet holes. Operating from Bernay, a formation of 17 Cyclones took off around 14.00hr for a routine patrol. On the way back from their mission they encountered several formations of bombers and fighters alike, in the Vernon and Melun sectors. With most of their wireless sets unserviceable, the leader of the Polish formation could not give orders, but the Me-109s of a Dornier 17 escort were so promptly on their tail that such orders were completely useless. Three German fighters and one bomber went down, the latter, a Do-17, being the joint victim of Capt Wezelik, Lt Kowalski and Sgt Markiewicz. Three Cyclones failed to return to base, and those who did all bore traces of the dogfights. This was to be their swansong anyway, because the next day the remaining 11 Caudron Cyclones, being unserviceable due to the impossibility of carrying out maintenance (the Germans were approaching their base), had to be destroyed.

The remnants of the aircrews were scattered, some pilots being detached to the GCI/8 and II/1, others going to the Rochefort air base for conversion to the Bloch 152. As for the Polish fighter school of Lyon, commanded by Lt Col Pamula, this had in fact formed one of the many ELD or local defence squadrons, with Morane 406s, five of the Cyclones to this CIC and even an odd Dewoitine 501. On June 13th the Paris garrison and the 7th Army withdrew from the capital. South of it, at Auxerre, some of the retreating Groupes de Chasse, five of them, were gathered together. This represented almost 100 fighters, and by sheer luck the Germans were unaware of it. GCIII/2, one of the Curtis Hawk-equipped units there, took off around 11.00hr for a routine mission. The 18 Hawks were led by Cdt Geille, who, besides being a fighter pilot, had also formed France's first paratroop unit. Intercepting a formation of Stukas, Geille was jumped from behind by escorting Me-109s and had to jump for his life . . . Badly wounded, his place was taken by Capt Rougevin-Baville who would lead the unit from airfield to airfield until the end. On the other side of the country, at the air base of le Luc on the French Riviera, the GCIII/6 under Cdt Stehlin had taken up station to re-equip with Dewoitine 520s. They had picked up their aircraft straight from the factory at Toulouse where row upon row of these splendid fighters were just waiting to be flown away . . . This was some days past, and now on this June 13th a formation of Fiat Cr-42 biplanes appeared over their field.

Commandant Stehlin, who had just landed from a routine patrol, jumped towards the radiocar and instructed the pilots still in the air to look after the Italians. One of them, the Adjudant Le Gloan, quickly attacked the Fiats which, probably taken by surprise, were slow to react. Two fell victim to Le Gloan's guns, but this was certainly not enough for him, as he continued to chase the others. After scoring another two, he finished his ammunition on a sole Fiat Br-20 bomber. For this sortie Le Gloan was later promoted Second Lt. Another of the sorties of GCIII/6 against the Italians, was during an escort mission for the French navy, during the latter's bombardment of the port of Genoa.

It was on the night of June 13th that Léo 451 bombers of the Groupement de Bombardement No 11 of the ZOAS took part in one of the few bombing missions against Italy. Only one aircraft failed to return but another was destroyed during take-off. On the Franco-German front, 17 Glenn Martin 167s had been attacking motor transport near Bergicourt; four of them fell as victims of the German light flak. Two aircraft, badly damaged, had to be abandoned at Romilly. This action took place two days before the fall of Paris. With the worsening of the situation, and perhaps with the aim of attacking the Italians in mind, an order was given on June 14th to withdraw a great part of the bomber force to bases in North Africa. Point of departure was Marseille-Marignane. Other bomber formations were assembled at the Salon de Provence and Istres airfields to continue the battle till the very end. These included all the Breguet 693s of the assault bomber formations, and also some groups who still flew the Amiot 143s. In all 11 groups were to stay till the end, the last mission being flown on June 24th by Léo 451s of GB6: German pontoon bridges were their target on the Moirans Grenoble leg. Only four aircraft reached their target because of bad weather, but this also prevented the enemy fighters from getting off the ground. How rapid was the German advance at certain places is shown by the following incident:

On June 16th, with the enemy streaming towards the Loire, the GCIII/3, equipped with Dewoitine 520s, was one of those formations instructed to show the flag to the army. At 12.55hr they took off to patrol the Auxerre-Tonnerre-Avalon sector. Flying over Auxerre, they noticed some French aeroplanes which were refuelling. Shooting down a Henschel 126 in the course of their flight, they turned towards Auxerre again, shortly after 14.00hr. Approaching at low level, one of the pilots, Sergeant Le Nigen, suddenly informed the leader that he had recognised several Henschel 126s over the airfield. One was promptly shot down during take-off, and the French returned to strafe their former airfield, destroying another three. Incidentally, this was the last operational sortie flown by Le Nigen, who, as a sergeant, had shot down 12 enemy aircraft in the space of one month. He was one of France's leading aces, but died in hospital in Morocco in July from appendicitis. A few days before, General d'Harcourt, C-in-C of the fighter arm, had awarded him the 'médaille militaire'.

On June 17th an order issued from the same General d'Harcourt instructed that most of the Dewoitine, Curtiss and Bloch-equipped fighter groups should prepare to leave for North Africa so as not to fall into enemy hands, and continue the battle. From the BBC studio B.2 in London, during the late afternoon of June 18th, 1940, a young Brigadier-General, named Charles de Gaulle, urged the French nation to continue the struggle on the side of Britain and the free world. Although most of the Armée de l'Air crews were too busy to have heard this speech, some did, and others were told about it shortly afterwards. The result was to come later, and come it did . . .

In the meantime, the first of the fighter groups ordered to the other side of the Mediterranean, left Perpignan, or Bordeaux for airfields situated in Algeria. Their ground crews, or at least some of them, embarked at the ports of Marseille, Port-Vendres, etc. Most of them without charts, with compasses not swung properly, with engines sometimes worn out due to the recent war missions, they flew away to a new destination. Many incidents took place during these flights over the sea. One pilot, a member of a formation of Curtiss Hawks led by a Bloch 174, suddenly found himself in heavy mist.

The Bloch 174 leading aircraft turned for base again, and in doing so, hit the fin and rudder of the Curtiss. With very heavy controls, the pilot of this fighter nevertheless pressed on and managed to reach Alger-Maison Blanche after a very strenuous flight. Another one, piloting a Dewoitine 520, had engine trouble shortly after crossing the Baleares Islands. Being in no mood to seek internment by the Spanish, he pressed

Maids of all work, the large number of Caudron C. 635M Simouns in service were either used for training purposes or communication duties with liaison flights such as the SAE (Sections d'Avions Estafette). One hundred and ten were ordered for the AA and many civilian aircraft of the same type were also impressed into service. Pictured here is a Simoun with s/n 140.

on, gradually losing height. Each time his engine came back to normal rpm he succeeded in gaining a few metres. He nevertheless managed to reach the coast of Algiers and ditched a few hundred metres from the beach.

From the 20th to the 24th the reconnaissance groupes able to do so, followed the bombers and fighters who had preceded them to North Africa. Thus a number of Potez 63-11s and Bloch 174s were saved from capture, as on June 22nd at 18.42hr, General Huntziger signed the armistice on behalf of the French government. This was not the end of all operations, as it had been understood that hostilities would have to cease with Italy before the armistice became valid.

Thus the old Amiot 143 bombers of GBI/38 were in the breech till the very end. It was only bad weather which prevented them from bombing German formations near Lyon on the 21st, or Genoa on the 22nd. On the 23rd, some of the remaining fighter formations undertook strafing missions against troops approaching Grenoble and Chambery, but their armament did not even damage the armour of the German tanks. Even the remnants of the night fighter squadrons were ordered to fly such missions, but boggy terrain and bad weather prevented most of their attempted take-offs. Only an aircraft of ECNI/13 and some of the ECN3/13 took to the air.

On June 24th, at around 18.00hr two sections of Morane 406s from the GCI/6 took off from their base at Marseille-Marignane. Their mission was to destroy enemy armoured units in the Romans, Beaurepaire sector. One of the sections, led by a Warrant Officer, succeeded in knocking out a flak battery, whilst the one led by Second Lt Raphenne went down to strafe German trucks standing in the main square of Beaurepaire village. Receiving a direct hit during one of his attacks this officer crashed his aircraft nearby. He was to be the last member of the air force killed during the battle of France. Four hours later, the armistice with Italy and Germany became valid. Lt Raphenne was buried by the Germans with full military honours at Mours.

Aftermath and Conclusions

It was often argued in different quarters, that if the battle of France had been lost, this was due in large measure to the lack of air support the army received from the Armée de l'Air. It was also argued that France's air force was decidedly inferior in quantity and quality to that of the Luftwaffe. Many people criticised the air force overall, citing its non-appearance over the front line. This latter point can be flatly refuted for the following reasons:

In aircrew alone, the Armée de l'Air lost approximately 1,490 men, of which 530 were wounded. It lost an estimated 1,200 aircraft, in air battles and due to actions on the ground, accidents, enemy bombing, etc. These figures are only approximate ones, for the good reason that many official records were lost during the latter stages of the campaign. From the figures available up to June 11th it is interesting to note that 250 fighters were lost in combat, against 123 due to accidents of all sorts, and another 135 due to enemy bombing operations. Bomber losses were 106 shot down, 43 written-off due to bombing actions and 70 due to accidents. As for the observation and reconnaissance planes, the figures are particularly relevant. Fifty-seven shot down, 56 destroyed due to bombing and 53 written-off because of accidents. Of course these figures do not correspond with those given during this period by the OKW. On the other hand, the French fighter arm claimed 813 victories, of which 585 were definitely confirmed.

If the air force had been absent, then these figures would not exist. The Armée de l'Air was present, but it was probably the way it operated which can eventually be criticised. No blame for this can be given to their gallant aircrews. To refute again the argument that, 'our pilots were never seen', let it be known how many French aircraft were destroyed over Belgian territory alone, during the campaign from May 10th to 28th, 1940. These comprised 29 Morane 406s, nine Bloch 152s, three Dewoitine 520s, seven Curtiss Hawks, one Léo 451, eight Breguet 693s (as related in this book), and seven Potez of the 631/63-11 family. This did not even include those aircraft which were shot down over Belgium, or crashed over the border.

As for the quantity of aircraft available, it is perhaps a sad statement to confirm, that the strength of the Armée de l'Air at the end of operations on June 25th was certainly superior to its strength at the start of the war in September 1939.

For example, there were the following aircraft in France in the part of the country under German control alone:

Morane 406:	453	Dewoitine 520:	170	Bloch 151:	51
Bloch 152:	260	Curtiss Hawk:	45	Potez 631:	112
Amiot 351/354:	8	Breguet 691:	49	Breguet 693:	43
Léo 451:	183	Glenn Martin 167:	13		
Bloch 174:	11	Potez 63-11:	221		

These figures did not include those aircraft that had already departed for North Africa. As far as the 'occupied zone' and 'non-occupied zone' is concerned, it should be noted that after the armistice and according to the agreements made with the Vichy government, the German forces withdrew from certain parts of their ultimate line of advance. These figures do not of course include those aircraft in service in other colonies.

One thing is certain, and that is that the argument of a deceptive rate of aircraft production cannot be withheld. The testimonies of pilots, who at the end of the campaign saw rows and rows of fighters or bombers on such and such an airbase are too well known. Whatever these were worth, it is an established fact that between May 10th, 1940 and June 12th 1,131 new aircraft were delivered to maintenance units and front line squadrons alike. These figures came from records of the EAA301 (the main delivery unit of new aircraft). These comprised 668 fighters, 355 bombers and 108 reconnaissance aircraft. If one compares these figures with the losses stated and also takes into account that of the destroyed aircraft, many were of older types, whilst their replacements were modern aircraft, it can be deduced that the aircraft industry had done its best.

The argument of sabotage in the rear can thus not be taken too seriously, although there had been some cases like the ones found during inquiries into the crashes of several NC (Hanriot) 232 advanced trainers. One thing was certain, Germany had first started her re-armament from 1934 onwards. The economic and political situation in France meant that only after 1936 had there been a start, albeit a small one, with her re-armament. Before the nationalisation of the aircraft industry, the means available were just enough to build 300 aircraft a year. With an albeit long reorganisation, and with money available at last, aircraft output rose gradually from 1938 onwards. During the battle of France it had reached a peak of nearly 300 aircraft per month. One thing is certain if some of the huge sums voted in the thirties for the navy had gone to the Armée de l'Air, the story might have been different.

What can certainly be blamed, is the way the army high command made use of the air force. Most of the army generals had the myth of the continuous front in mind, and even with double the strength of the air force available, they still would have made poor use of it. It is told, for example, that from June 1st to 4th, 1940, the force of Breguet 693 assault bombers, and their fighter escorts, were never called upon by the army corps for which they were destined to operate. The superior tactics of the German army, the better use it made of the panzer/observation/bomber team made this campaign doomed to failure. What the air force could have improved on was its use of the bomber arm, the co-ordination/liaison between air force and army (the later 2nd Tactical Air Force in Europe was an example of how things should have been) and the solving of maintenance problems at the rear. The gallantry of its air and ground-crews certainly could not be in doubt.

2 | *Survival and Revival*

In the early morning of June 25th, three pilots of the GCIII/7, aided by a few ground-crew, prepared themselves for a somewhat special mission, which had not been notified in the squadron's ops room. Having received their brand new Dewoitine 520 fighters in exchange for battle-weary Moranes only a few days before, the three took off under very bad weather conditions and set course from Toulouse to England, where they arrived in the neighbourhood of Portsmouth. One of the pilots was Adjudant Littolf, better known for his later career with the 'Normandie-Niemen' Regiment. The three pilots were but the first of a steady flow who joined the 'Free French' created by General de Gaulle. On July 3rd, 1940, a large formation of Curtiss Hawks of both GCI/5 and II/5 were patrolling over the Mediterranean near Oran and the naval base of Mers-el-Kébir to protect the French fleet against attacks from the Fleet Air Arm.

These two incidents illustrate the sad fact that, from the armistice onwards, and this till the early days of the Allied landings in North Africa in 1942, there were in fact two French air forces, one, the Armée de l'Air de l'Armistice, better known as the Vichy Air Force, and the other, the Forces Aériennes Françaises Libres with HQ in London, and better known as the Free French Air Force. Although many of the former were on the side of the Allies, and some of them succeeded in joining the FAFL ranks, others obeyed only the given word and, disciplined as they were, gave their lives for a wrong cause.

Undeniably the bigger of the two, for obvious reasons, the Vichy air force could muster the following types of aircraft after the armistice. These figures cannot be considered as definitive, but will at least give the reader an idea of what this air arm could put into operation. Even if, from the onset of the armistice, Hitler had agreed to allow the Vichy government some sort of armed forces including an air force, this for strictly political reasons, it was the British attack on the fleet at Mers-el-Kébir which gave the French definite arguments for re-arming their existing units, and to urge the German-Italian control committee for more freedom of action and more equipment. Five groups of Dewoitine D520s formed the better part of the interception force. These were GCI/3, II/3, III/3, III/6 and II/7, which could muster around 165 aircraft. Five other units accounted for 146 Curtiss Hawks, but two of them, the GCIII/2 and II/4 were disbanded in August of the same year The others, GCI/5 and II/5 were stationed in Morocco, GCI/5 at Rabat-Salé and GCII/5 at Casablanca. Prior to these airfields, they had been near Oran (Saint Denis du Sig) in Algeria. Four groups were equipped with Morane 406s, of which one, GCI/7 was at Rayak in

Glenn Martin 167 of the 'Armée de l'Air de l'Armistice' better known as the Vichy Air Force. This picture taken in North Africa shows a line up of such bombers, which served with the Vichy Air Force as follows: GB 1/39 in Syria, GB 1/62 and 1/63 in Mali at Bamako, GB 11/62 and 11/63 at Thies in Senegal and GR 1/22 a recce unit at Rabat-Sale in Morocco.

Syria, the others in North Africa. In total there were 200 of these fighters still available, including those in maintenance units, and small fighter detachments such as EC2/565 on the island of Madagascar. There was even one unit, GCIII/4 which still had the elderly Dewoitine D510s. Eleven of these fighters were still in unoccupied France at this time, but were written-off as scrap later on when the Germans invaded this part of the country.

A considerable number of bombing units were also stationed in North Africa. Amongst them were five fully equipped with Léo 451s and one a mixed unit with Léo 451s and obsolete Bloch 210s. Another group had the even older Léo 257bis which dated from the late twenties or early thirties period. In total there were 135 Léo 451s accounted for outside France. As for the Glenn Martin 167s, a grand total of 200 were available. These were scattered all over the 'Empire', GBI/39 in Syria, GBI/62 and I/63 at Bamako (Mali) and GBII/62 and II/63 at Thiès (Senegal). The other American-designed bomber which served with the Vichy air force was the Douglas DB7, of which 95 were available, some still in their crates.

Four groupes were equipped with these, amongst them GBI/19 and I/32. Thirty-five of the Amiot 351/354 bombers belonging to GBI/21 and II/21 and some mixed units were also available, although not much is known of their operations. The older Farman 222, the only four-engined bombers of the Armée de l'Air, were also available in some quantities, their former bombing role being changed into that of long range transport. Their original unit was renamed GTII/15 (GT for Groupe de Transport) in November 1940, and during the Vichy period they were to be seen all over the 'Empire'. One small squadron of them was even based as far away as Indo-China and the independent group GAA43, at Thiès in Senegal, also had five of them on strength.

In the Levant there was even an escadrille of six Bloch 200 bombers, based at Baalbek (Lebanon), taken over from GBI/39 who, as stated above, had been re-equipped with Martin 167s. Several of the old Potez 540 multi-purpose bombers of the mid-thirties also served with the Armée de l'Air de l'Armistice, mostly in the transport role. In the transport and communications role, many of the Caudron Goëlands, Caudron Simouns, Dewoitine D338s and others left in the occupied zone of France, were also taken on strength by Vichy. Its most modern trainer was certainly the North American NAA-57, of which 100 at least served in North Africa. Those still in unoccupied France are not included in this figure. In the category of 'ancestors' can also be included the Potez 25 TOE (Théatre d'Opérations Etranger) or in English, 'for overseas service'. A great number of these operated with several GAO and local station flights, etc. In the reconnaissance role, the Bloch 174 and 175 formed the 'elite' and GRII/33 at its base at Tunis-el-Aouina (Tunisia) had at least 13 of them (MB174). The other recipient of the rather more up-to-date Bloch 175s was GRII/52 at Oran-la Sénia (Algeria). In total, 35 of these recce Blochs were available in July 1940. Such groups as GRI/22 at Rabat (Morocco), GRI/36 at Sétif (Algeria) GRII/39 at Damas (Syria) and the GAOI/583 at Aleppo, had the proven Potez 63-11. Later on GRI/22 and probably still another reconnaissance unit were partially re-equipped with Glenn Martin 167s.

As for the elements in active service in the unoccupied zone of France, one can mention several Bloch 152 and Bloch 155 groupes de chasse, six in total, with a statutory strength of 24 aircraft each. Amongst them were GCI/8 and II/8. There were also a number of Potez 631s of the former night fighter squadrons left operational in this part of France. They formed the backbone of the air defence of Vichy France, made up of two sectors, one for the south-east and one for the south-west. Each of these sectors comprised a number of fighter groups with bases at Le Luc, Marignane and Salon de Provence for the former, and Montpellier and Nimes for the latter. Two fighter groups (GCI/1 and II/9) were retained at Lyon and Aulnat as general reserve.

All these units, with the exception of a night fighter squadron of Potez 631s which was moved to Gabès (Tunisia) in the summer of 1941, were disbanded when German forces invaded the unoccupied zone in November 1942. By that time many of these French-based groupes de chasse had been re-equipped with Dewoitine D520 fighters. It should be noted that these were brand new aircraft, as the Vichy government had made agreements with the RLM in Berlin which permitted the French aircraft industry to continue production of certain indigenous types for its own use in the so-called 'zone libre' or free zone of France, whilst those industries situated in the occupied zone were to build German-designed types for the Luftwaffe.

Amongst these were 150 Léo 451s out of an order of 225, an order which was granted by the Germans to the Vichy authorities. These bombers were constructed at the Ambérieu plant of the then SNCASE, the Germans even going so far as to return all the spare parts found in their occupied zone.

Other aircraft built in this part of France were Bloch 155s at the Châteauroux factory, and over 300 Dewoitine 520s at the Toulouse factory of the SNCASE.

As for the operations of the Armée de l'Air de l'Armistice against her former allies, these can be resumed as follows:

On July 3rd, 1940 units of the Royal Navy, known as 'Force H' attacked the French fleet at anchor off Mers-al-Kébir. The Curtiss Hawks of GCI/5 and II/5 were ordered to intercept any aircraft of the Fleet Air Arm which might attack the French vessels. Although a fierce battle was raging on the ground, the two former allies were probably in the same state of mind and one pilot of II/5 relates that his, and the British formation, flew parallel with each other, maintaining their distance, and after a while the British broke away towards their carrier. Another unit, however, was attacked by Blackburn Skuas and one of these was shot down. As history now knows, this political blunder, the action being carried out with the utmost reluctance on the part of the Royal Navy, had for result that many a pilot, who had the firm intention of escaping to fight in Britain, refrained from doing so. In others it occasioned such a state of mind that future clashes in the air would be fought with very much more vigour.

In reprisal, Vichy air force Douglas DB7s of GBI/32 attacked Gibraltar, but with little result.

In the meantime, another operation was prepared, with the aim of landing Free French forces at the important port of Dakar. Known as 'Opération Menace' the British and Free French combined task force attacked on September 23rd and two French-piloted light observation planes even took off from HMS *Ark Royal* and landed at the aerodrome of Ouakam for a goodwill mission. They did not come back . . . but Glenn Martin 167 bombers of a unit stationed at Dakar bombed the

Left: Displaying full Vichy air force markings, on engine cowlings and fins and tailplane, this Potez 63-11 with individual serial No 6 belonged to a unit based in North Africa. In November 1941 the Vichy Air Force had 236 of these aircraft on strength besides a hundred of the older types of the 630, 631 and 637 variety. **Below:** Out of 316 Curtiss Hawk 75 fighters taken on charge by the Armée de l'Air, 146 were able to cross the Mediterranean on the eve of the armistice in July, about forty plus, unserviceable machines remaining in the free zone of France. The north African-based aircraft belonged to five groupes de chasse, saw action for the first time again, against their former allies during the British attack on the naval base of Mers El Kebir in July 1940. Amongst the victims of the GC I/5 and II/5 were various Blackburn Skuas of the Fleet Air Arm.

Allied ships. The operation was not continued, but the Vichy forces retaliated again on Gibraltar.

The next operation of the Vichy air force was to be in a totally different theatre, although about the same period. When the 5th Japanese Army (Army of Canton) attacked French positions in the Langson region on September 22nd, 1940, three Potez 631s which had been in crates destined for the Chinese air force, were hastily put in service to reconnoitre the Japanese lines of penetration. Afterwards they were put back in their crates, as no official permission had been obtained to use them!

From December 1940 till January 22nd, 1941 there had been a state of war with Thailand (Siam). This came about because of the latter country's intention of annexing part of Cambodia and Laos. The whole French air force in Indo-China could muster about 100 aircraft, of which only 20 Morane 406 fighters could be considered modern. There were also some Farman F.222 bomber transports, and during these operations against the Thai forces, there was amongst others a Potez 631 belonging to the GAM42 (Groupement Aérien Mixte), which operated from Siem-Reap. The Thai air force which, as opposed to the French, had been supplied with more or less modern aircraft of American origin, could be considered the larger of the two. Nevertheless, it was successes achieved by the French navy that halted these operations. The next clash of Vichy aircraft was during operation 'Ironclad', when Allied forces landed on May 6th, 1942 at Diego-Suarez in Madagascar. Although these landings were intended to prevent Japanese influence in the Indian Ocean, rather than against Vichy, this did not change the fact that the French fought bitterly and only on November 5th did they capitulate. At Ivato-Tananarive there had been the Escadrille de Renseignements 555 (recce sq 555) with Potez 63-11s. By February 1942 it had merged with the Morane 406-equipped Escadrille de Chasse I/565 to form a Groupe Aérien Mixte at Ivato with a detachment at Diego-Suarez. In the operations against the Sea Hurricanes and Albacores from HMS *Illustrious* and HMS *Indomitable* and South African air force Beauforts, four Potez 63-11s were lost. The same happened to the Morane 406 which claimed a couple of victories. All four of them were destroyed when the cease-fire came into being.

A very different sort of operation was the one known as the Syrian Campaign and which had taken place from May 15th to July 15th, 1941.

The official reason for its start had been the identification of German aircraft on bases in Syria, but the main reason was certainly the facilities allowed by Vichy for the transit of German weapons to the Iraqi pro-German rebels, and the fact that ever since Versailles, the British had always looked upon the French mandate of Syria and Lebanon as a thorn in their flesh. Also taken into account was the fact that General de Gaulle was only too keen to annex this part of the empire to the cause of the 'Free French' for obvious reasons. Hostilities opened in fact on May 15th, when a Bristol Blenheim IVF escorted by Curtiss Tomahawks from 250 sq. strafed the airfield of Palmyra. Due to the RAF being heavily committed with the Iraqi affair, the air activity was rather weak, No 11 sq. taking over from No 84 with a handful of Blenheims. At the start of the campaign, French forces were principally a GCI/7 with a statutory strength of 26 Morane 406 fighters. Further available were the usual Potez 25 TOE which served in five Groupes Aériens de Recon-

Left: This Dewoitine D.520 of GC II/3 from Maison Blanche, Algeria, belonged to a unit which saw action against the Allies during the Syrian campaign, the 4th escadrille of GC II/3. Note the individual aircraft number 28 along the fuselage. **Above:** The only resident fighter unit at the start of the Allied attack on Syria and the Lebanon, was the Morane 406 equipped GC I/7, aircraft of which are seen here at Rayak in Syria.

This Leo 451 bomber of GB 1/25 seen flying here over the town of Tunis belonged to one of several such equipped units which the Germans had permitted to remain operational. GB 1/25 took part in the Syrian campaign against the Allies and of 18 aircraft, 12 were lost.

naissance (GAO) at Baalbek, Aleppo, Rayak, Palmyra and Deir-ez-Zor. At Aleppo there was another GAO equipped with modern Potez 63-11s. On May 28th, 1942, a Morane 406 claimed a victory over a Blenheim near Aleppo. During an escort of Ju-52 transports by other Morane 406 fighters the former's air gunners, who had probably never taken part in the battle of France, or were not very proficient in aircraft recognition, almost had the dubious honour of shooting down their own escorts. The same day, the air defence of the Levant was strengthened by Dewoitine 520 fighters of GCIII/6. Whatever the number of German aircraft in transit through Syria had been, none were left by May 31st. On June 5th it was the turn of the Regia Aeronautica to support the visit of the RAF. On June 7th Morane 406s intercepted a Hurricane of 208 sq. but managed only to damage it slightly. On June 8th the war began in earnest when British, Free French, Indian and Australian troops crossed the border. Air support for these operations came not only from the RAF but also from the Fleet Air Arm. From the start of the offensive, the Glenn Martin 167s of GBI/39 bombed Allied troop concentrations near Quneitra and Dewoitine D520s flew escort to Potez 63-11 recce aircraft. Tomahawks of 3 sq. RAAF strafed Rayak damaging some D520s and a 208 sq. RAF Hurricane was shot down by Second Lt Le Gloan's Dewoitine, adding another aircraft to this ace's score, albeit one of a different nationality than the ones he used to down during the battle of France. Who said politics was too serious a matter to be taken up by the military?

The opposing Fairey Fulmars of the FAA squadron involved (803 sq) were no match for the Dewoitines who claimed several of them. On the

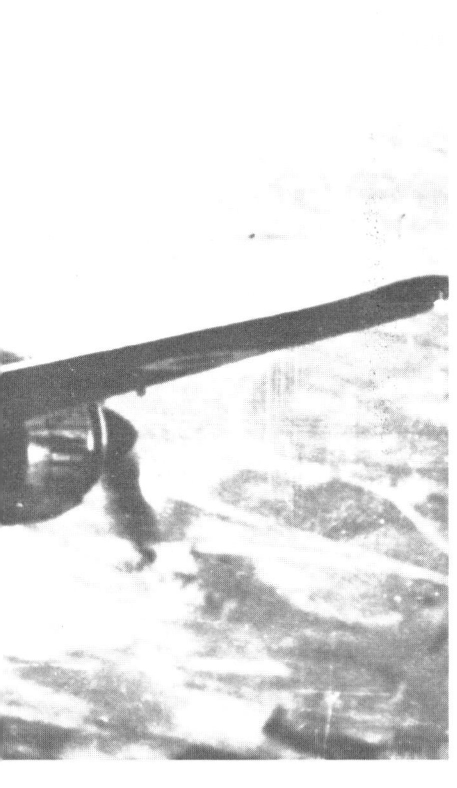

9th the French attacked British warships near Saida with a mixed formation of Glenn Martin 167 and Bloch 200 bombers, escorted by Dewoitine 520s. If the Hurricanes of 80 sq made easy meat out of the Bloch 200s, which either blew up or crash-landed like the one at Beirut, they themselves fell victim to some of the Dewoitines and lost some of their number, but not before a couple of D520s also went down, one of them colliding with a Hurricane in mid-air. GBI/31 was the first of three Léo 451-equipped units which appeared as reinforcement for the French. It arrived on June 11th. On the 12th Morane 406s strafed an Allied camp at Deraa and a No 11 sq RAF Blenheim was lost to a Dewoitine of GCIII/6

On June 15th French forces counter-attacked and retook Quneitra. Their air elements had received some other reinforcements in the meantime, in the form of GBI/25 with Léo 451s and GCII/3 with Dewoitine 520s, the latter unit from Tunis. GBI/12 was the other Léo 451 bombing group available. During a mission of D520s, these encountered Gloster Gladiators of which several were shot down, but the old biplanes had defended themselves well and one D520 was shot down, while another crash-landed. On June 18th Gladiators of 'X' Flight even managed to score two kills in a dogfight with Dewoitines, the two French pilots belonging to GCIII/6. This action took place over Kissoué. During night missions the French even operated the old Potez 25 TOE biplanes, these seeing action at Sanamein and Artouz amongst other places. With the fall of Damascus on the 21st the French concentrated on a column of some 800 vehicles, known as the 'Habforce' and which had entered the country from Iraq.

These were seriously strafed by Moranes from GCI/7 during June 23rd and 24th. It was on the 23rd that the Allies made an all-out effort to wipe out as many French planes as possible. In this, Hurricanes of the RAF and Tomahawks of the RAAF were very successful, no fewer than 25 French planes being destroyed at one base. These ranged from the Potez 63-11 to the Farman 222 via the Glenn Martin 167. At the end of the month the Vichy French still had the following aircraft available, not including those of the Aéronavale. Eleven Dewoitine 520s, 12 Morane 406s, 17 Léo 451s, and only three Glenn Martins. A handful of Potez 63-11s, some Farman four-engined bomber-transports of the F222 family and other older aircraft like Potez 25 TOEs, etc, made up the total. That the French pilots and aircrews did not give up was shown on July 3rd when, during an escort mission to Léo 451s over Deir-ez-Zor, they destroyed three Hurricanes of 127 sq who had dived on this mixed formation. One of the British fighters had collided with a Léo 451, but the bomber managed to fly back to base. A tribute to French maintenance personnel was the fact that the number of serviceable aircraft in one or other category was augmented in comparison to the ones available on the last day of June. An uncommon feat happened on the night of July 7th when Adjudant Chef Armager of GCI/7 managed to shoot down a Blenheim at night (00.25hr). However, it was now only too clear that the Vichy forces were about to give up. On the 8th the road from Damascus to Palmyra was open for Allied motor transport. Those French air force units who could, evacuated to the island of Rhodes, the very successful GCIII/6 flying back to Alger-Maison Blanche. Of the units that stayed till the end there were the

GCI/7, because their Moranes lacked the range to fly across the Mediterranean. GCII/3 with Dewoitine D520s and the Léo 451 equipped GBI/25 also stayed as did the Aéronavale units.

On July 9th RAF Hurricanes damaged practically all the Farman F222 transports of GTII/15. On the 11th, 12 Dewoitine 520s of GCII/3, who had set course for a sweep on Palmyra, encountered a mixed formation of Tomahawks and Hurricanes *en route* for the same sort of mission over the Aleppo region. In the resulting dogfights, both parties lost some of their aircraft, the French continuing to strafe Palmyra with nine D520s where they destroyed several Gladiators on the ground, as well as a Westland Lysander. The French having asked for terms, the last French bombing mission was flown in the afternoon of July 12th by some Léo 451s of the GBI/25. It left the country the next day. With 13 Dewoitine D520s out of the 23 it had at the start of operations, the GCII/3 left in turn for its home base in Tunisia. In all, this had been a bitterly fought campaign, and for many of the French aircrew who had taken part it was still not the end of their troubles.

The Allies had been preparing a huge landing operation along the Algerian and Moroccan coast, and to this end, secret contacts had been made with some of the French military and political leaders there. Unfortunately, when these landings, known as 'Operation Torch' started on November 8th, 1942, it was far from certain that these pro-Allied leaders would neutralise the French forces stationed there. For several reasons, such as the general war situation, the fact that the Americans were on the side of the Allies, and because a great number of the military were only too keen 'd'en découdre', ie to take their revenge

for the German victory of 1940, they too hoped that their leaders would be on the Allied side. As it turned out, things went rather well in Algeria, but the high command in Morocco had other thoughts, and it was there that most of the unnecessary bloodshed took place. The main units of the Vichy air force in Morocco were the GCI/5 at Rabat-Salé, with Curtiss Hawks and Dewoitine 520s, and GCII/5 at Casablanca also with Curtiss Hawks but starting to re-equip with the Dewoitine 520s. Two bomber units had the Léo 451 (GBI/23 at Marrakesh and GBII/23 at Meknès) whilst another two had Douglas DB7s, one at Casablanca and the other operating from Rabat-Salé. Also based at Rabat were Farman F222 bomber transports of GTI/15.

When morning dawned upon the city the alert had been sounded for the pilots of GCII/5 and nine of their number were patrolling Casablanca harbour when the battleship *Jean-Bart* suddenly opened fire in response to gunfire from American vessels. Soon afterwards the French formation was attacked by a formation of US navy aircraft diving towards the ships at anchor. During one of these fighter-bomber attacks, a young sergeant had followed them, thinking, as he said afterwards, that they were simply overflying the ships as a friendly gesture. 'When I saw them suddenly dropping their bombs, I realized what was going on, and opened fire on the nearest of them, scoring a direct hit. I never thought the Americans would have done this' . . . In 15 minutes of aerial combat, eight pilots of GCII/5 had been killed, one of them after coming down with his Curtiss, had jumped into an available Dewoitine 520 and had crashed on take-off, his propeller being in coarse pitch. A little later, two pilots appeared at the base, one helping the other to walk.

Left: This fine air shot of a Vichy Potez 63-11 displays again the markings used during this period. **Below:** One of several reconnaissance groups operating the Potez 63-11 in North Africa prior to the Allied landings, GR 1/52 aircraft shown here are flying on a routine mission over the Rif territory of Morocco.

One was a French pilot, who had downed the other, an American naval pilot, shortly before the Frenchman was himself shot down . . . Asked if he knew the nationality of his opponent, the American replied, 'I thought they were Germans . . .'.

Not everywhere did the fortunes of war result in such encounters and at Oran for example, the allied forces destroyed the whole of GRII/52's Bloch 174s. The same fate befell most of the bomber units, and on the next day, November 9th, Admiral of the Fleet Darlan ordered a cease fire. Two days later the Wehrmacht invaded the non-occupied zone of France, and all Vichy air units were disbanded, their aircraft being taken over by the Luftwaffe or distributed to such countries as Roumania, Finland, etc.

Thus the Armée de l'Air de l'Armistice terminated its short existence, the only positive result being that many of its fully-trained pilots were very keen, and able to continue the battle alongside the Allied forces, and this they did with great success. With the 'Free French' units of de Gaulle they merged into a newly created 'Armée de l'Air'. As for the 'Forces Aériennes Françaises Libres' or 'Free French Air Force' this is how their story began.

As related previously, three Dewoitine 520 fighters had escaped from Toulouse to fly to Britain on June 25th, 1940, only a few days after the memorable BBC speech of de Gaulle. They were not the first to do so, because on the 14th, a young NCO named Demozay, who had previously served as interpreter to the RAF in France, took off with an abandoned British bomber and, in company of a mixed bunch of British and French, succeeded in bringing his aircraft down near London. He ended the war as a fully fledged pilot, On June 18th, day of de Gaulle's famous speech, three Caudron Simoun liaison aircraft took off from Royan, bringing another five pilots for the Allied cause. On the 20th a Farman F222 took off for Saint Eval with 18 NCOs and one officer. On the 24th at least 30 young members of the Ecole de l'Air, some officers and NCOs embarked at Port Vendres *en route* to Gibraltar. Landing at Ismailia in Egypt on June 27th, Péronne lead a section of three Morane 406 fighters from Rayak, with very old orders to put his unit at the disposal of the RAF. This was followed by a Potez 63-11 from the same base. On July 3rd a small cargo vessel, the *Président Houduce* left Gibraltar for Britain. On board was Sgt René Mouchotte who, with a number of other French air force types, had landed there with a Caudron Goëland some days before. He took off from Oran with an aircraft whose propeller pitch had been sabotaged deliberately, so as to avoid pilots taking off. With constant night patrols by cars using full headlights and with guards all over the field, they had managed to escape to freedom. Mouchotte was later to become CO of 341 Squadron, RAF, better known to the French as the Groupe de Chasse 'Alsace'. In Egypt again, two Glenn Martin 167 (RAF Maryland) bombers, together with the above-mentioned aircraft, formed the first 'Free French' flight ready for operations. A Caudron Simoun with two pilots on board followed the same day as Mouchotte's landing. Three Glenn Martin bombers arrived also, but one of them was destroyed by Spanish anti-aircraft guns during its final approach and it crashed into the harbour. The four crew were killed. In September, one of Coastal Command's future aces, Max Guedj, embarked at Tanger. From places as far away as Indo-China

Right: Second from right, in front of a Spitfire, is the late Commandant Rene Mouchotte, the first CO of the groupe de chasse 'Alsace' (341 Sqn, RAF) when it started operations from the UK. On the extreme left is Lt Duperier, who took over for a short while after Mouchotte's death on August 27th, 1943. **Below right:** Seen here in the cockpit of his Hawker Hurricane is Lt Duperier, one of a handful of French pilots who joined the RAF from the start and saw service with 242 Sqn and 615 Sqn.

and South America, they came to join de Gaulle's FAFL. Others left occupied France in fishing boats, like Jacques Andrieux, a future pilot of 130 sq, or by plane, like Maurice Halna du Fretay, who managed to take off from his parents' estate with a Zlinn he had completely rebuilt. The future chief of staff of the FAFL, General Martial Valin, came from as far away as Brazil, where he had been appointed 'Air Attaché' in 1940, having served during the phoney war with the GRI/33. Bernard Duperier, later one of the first commanding officers of the GC 'Ile de France', came with some fellow pilots like Corniglion-Molinier from a trip which had nearly taken them round the world. As for Captain Tulasne, he simply disappeared from Rayak in Syria with one of GCI/7's Morane 406s and joined the RAF in Egypt. He was to be one of the future aces and CO of the 'Normandie-Niemen' fighter regiment. It was not only aircrew who had this urge for freedom. Dr. Georges Lebiendinsky, a Russian-born young medical officer who later served in the 'Normandie-Niemen' unit, travelled via Portugal and the USA before finally reaching London and the Free French. Taking into account the extreme difficulties which had to be supported by most of its future members, it is understandable that it took several months, even a couple of years, to form these various FAFL units which one knows so well.

After passing through 'Patriotic School', the then well-known trials centre for every new arrival in the UK and with some unhappy experience of the reception committee there, the future candidate for RAF wings was either sent to an IFTS or straight to an OTU, according to his qualifications or his good luck. From there, future fighter pilots made the acquaintance of the Hawker Hurricane, while others went on Avro Ansons and Vickers Wellingtons before joining French units and other equipment. From the very beginning of the FAFL, however, some pilots had taken the air in British skies. At Saint Athan, in Wales, there were no less than ten former Armée de l'Air aircraft which, overpainted with RAF markings, and with the traditional yellow undersides, were flown by French crews for practice training, that is, as long as the spares were available. These planes ranged from the sleek Dewoitine 520 (three) to the elderly four-engined Farman F222 bomber (one) or the Potez 63-11 (two). Meantime, the Battle of Britain was going on, and five French pilots took an active part in this historic battle. On the other side of the Mediterranean, two former Vichy AF Glenn Martins bearing the s/n 82 and 102, had fled the régime, leaving their base in Tunisia for Aden, where they formed the first Free French Flight. This happened on July 13th, 1940. A second Free French Flight was formed apparently on July 8th, 1940, again in the Middle East, and it saw operations from July 20th onwards under Captain Jacquier at Heliopolis. It consisted of at least seven Morane 406 fighters and two Potez 63-11 recce aircraft.

Left: A Morane 406, s/n 831, one of the few who escaped to serve with the RAF in the Middle East. It served alongside 274 Sqn at Amriya, later operating independently in Libya. Part of 'Free French Flight No 2' this unit can be considered as the origin of the famous GC 'Alsace'. When disbanded in September 1942, it moved to the UK and reformed on Spitfire Vbs in January 1943. (Note the Lorraine cross along the fuselage and under the wings.) **Above:** Taken during an operation in the Fezzan, this picture shows the crew of a crash-landed Glenn Martin 167. Note the squadron insignia in front of the cockpit. **Right:** Bristol Blenheim IV, no 18, belonged to the first 'Lorraine' squadron formed in Syria with the remnants of the escadrille 'Topic' and 'Menace' who had operated with Colonel Leclerc's forces. From November 1941 till April 1942 it flew in support of British forces during the latter's offensive in Cyrenaica.

From August 19th, 1940 onwards, these operated with No 274 sq, RAF, who incidentally flew Gladiators at that time. By the end of September the French No 2 Flight left for Haifa in Palestine (now Israel) and operated in Lybia against the Italian forces. A third Flight, used in the communications and transport role, saw service on the Egypt–Palestine run.

Also in August was formed the Groupe de Combat No 1 under command of Lt Col Lionel de Marmier, the well-known pilot whose name had previously been linked with the Polish-manned GCI/145. This unit had left Liverpool, with Blenheim B Mk IVs, a couple of Dewoitine D520s and four Westland Lysanders. On August 1st, another French unit, known as the escadrille 'Topic' was formed under Captain Astier de Villatte. It had eight Blenheims on strength. It should be noted that the unit which had left Liverpool on August 25th was sometimes known to the French as the escadrille 'Menace'. When on August 26th the Tchad joined the forces of de Gaulle, the Potez-25 TOE and other Blochs available were named as the 'Détachement Permanent des Forces Aériennes du Tchad'. This was a rather pompous name for the number of aircraft available, but after the operations over

central Africa by the escadrille 'Topic's' Blenheims, these came under control of the Tchad detachment. From then on, the Détachment Permanent des Forces Aériennes du Tchad operated with Bristol Blenheim B Mk IVs, some Glenn Martin 167 Marylands and Westland Lysanders in support of Colonel Leclerc's forces which operated against the Italians and took part in operations in the Tibesti desert, Koufra and Mourzouk. It then went on further operations against Italian forces in Abyssinia. Moving afterwards to Syria, now occupied by Allied forces, it had on strength more than 20 Blenheim IV bombers. From November 1941 to April 1942 it flew in support of British forces in Cyrenaica. From November 1942 onwards, the French crews were sent back to England, and it was only on April 7th, 1943 that the newly-formed 342 'Lorraine' squadron was born at West Raynham, equipped with Douglas Bostons. It had received this name in September 1941 when still part of the Groupe de Reconnaissance et de Bombardement No 1 in far away Africa.

Meantime, back in Britain, the end of 1941 saw the birth of the first Free French fighter squadron (No 340 sq, RAF) as a completely independent formation. Formed at Turnhouse on Spitfire F Mk IIs in November 1941, it remained in Scotland until April 1942, took part in the Dieppe Commando raid in the same year, during which operation it scored its first confirmed victories. To the French this unit was known as the Groupe de Chasse 'Ile de France'. Amongst its commanding officers were such men as de Scitivaux, Duperier (later a President of the Aero-Club de France) and Schloesing. At the same RAF station, Turnhouse, a few years later (January 1st, 1943) was formed the second Free French Spitfire unit, known as 341 sq or Groupe de Chasse 'Alsace'. It flew Spitfire F Mk Vs till March when it re-equipped with Spitfire F Mk IXs. Its CO was the by then well-known Commandant Mouchotte, former Flight Commander at 615 sq (RAuxAF). Mouchotte led the squadron till his untimely death on August 27th, 1943. Amongst the members of this unit were men like Clostermann, who ended the war as France's top scorer, and had just started operations with the 'Alsace' sq shortly before Mouchotte's death. Commandant Dupérier took over afterwards. In the meantime, as early as November 1st, 1940 Sergeant Choron had scored the first aerial victory for the Free French when he shot down a Heinkel He-115 seaplane. On February 26th, 1941 Pilot Officer Lafont scored a first Free French hit over his home country, Second Lt Bouquillard being the first FAFL fighter pilot to be killed by the Luftwaffe. If the year 1941 had been the period of hope, 1942 was to be the year of consolidation.

Two important events took place during this period. First there was the desire of General de Gaulle to have a fighting unit of French nationality co-operating with the Russians in the Soviet Union, and secondly there was Operation 'Torch', the Allied landings in North Africa. The idea of having Frenchmen in the URSS was not new, as the former Vichy air attaché in Moscow, Colonel Luguet, who had rallied the Gaullist forces, had suggested this to the commanding officer of the FAFL, General Martial Valin. Contact was made with members of the Soviet embassy in London, with the approval of de Gaulle of course.

The results were that volunteers were recruited as early as August 1942 and despatched to Lagos in Nigeria from where a Belgian Airlines (Sabena) Junkers Ju-52 flew them to Cairo. From there they joined a

Above: Part of the Groupe de Combat No 1 formed in August 1940, this Westland Lysander was part of a mixed batch of aircraft, Blenheim B Mk IVs and Dewoitine D.520 included, which sailed from Liverpool. They operated in support of Colonel Leclerc's forces against the Italians in the Tibesti desert, Koufra and Mourzouk. Note the rugged terrain, and the upper wing camouflage of this Lysander not especially typical to the standard RAF camouflage.
Right: According to the fortunes of war, the FAFL were able to impress several aircraft which had belonged to either Vichy or French civilian airlines. This Dewoitine D 338 three-engined transport aircraft was one. Note the civilian registration FL-AQB underlined with tricoloured band, and the cross of Lorraine insignia on the fuselage underneath the cockpit.

party of other volunteers at Rayak and after a spell of rest at Teheran, 61 of them, ground-crew included, were flown in three Soviet Dakotas to Bakou. From there the trip continued for the night stop at Gouriev. Almost frozen to death, the whole party under Commandant Pouliquen, a veteran from 1917-18, and his deputy, Commandant Tulasne, arrived at Moscow, where after a small welcome party, they left for the training base of Ivanovo, 150km north-east of the capital. There they started training on the Yak-1. The Russians had proposed several types of western aircraft also, but Cdt Tulasne, in charge of flying training, adopted the Russian aircraft. This, and the fact that the Frenchmen arrived at a period far from favourable for the Soviet armies (the battle for Stalingrad was raging) made them from the onset very popular. In a totally different operational environment from what they had been accustomed to in the Middle East and Britain, they first had to learn the tricky way of flying continuously over snow-covered terrain. At first the UT-2 trainer biplane was their mount, followed by the dual control Yak-7 fighter trainer, with fixed undercarriage. Comfort and food were nothing in comparison to what they had been accustomed to in the Royal Air Force and only the kindness of the Russian people whom they met and the goodwill shown by their Soviet comrade in arms, enabled them to keep up their morale. Whilst their training continued, the North African skies witnessed other air battles favourable to the Allies and the FAFL. When the Vichy air forces had been wiped out most of the crews were only too keen to continue the fight alongside the Anglo-Americans, and thus all these aircraft which had been saved started operations against the common enemy. From the existing units, GBI/25 for example, were flown supply missions for the USAAF with its Léo 451s. One detachment of GBI/11 and the remaining aircraft from GBII/23 formed the Groupement Mixte No 8 from early 1943 onwards and undertook night bombing missions against German forces till April 1943, for the loss of only two aircraft. After a period of inactivity from May onwards, their crews embarked for Britain in August to re-form on British bombers. The Léo 451s were left to form the bomber OTU at

Left: This Glenn Martin 167 displaying clearly the cross of Lorraine insignia of the 'Free French' served with the 'Detachement permanent du Tchad' and took part in the Fezzan campaign under Colonel Leclerc. Some of these Marylands, as they were known in the RAF, were in fact aircraft from a a French contract taken over by the British. Some of these bombers belonged to the 'escadrille de bombardement No 2' formed in March 1941 at Brazaville. Other Glenn Martin 167s had fled from Vichy government-held territories formed the escadrille de bombardement No 1 (a very small unit in fact) and operated from Aden with the RAF against Italian possessions in East Africa during 1940.

Above right: Despite the fact that 94 Leo 451 bomber were seized by the Germans when they occupied Southern France in answer to the Allied landings in Algeria and Morocco, and others were destroyed during Allied raids, still others went on serving the Allied and Free French cause. GB 1/25's remaining Leo 451s were flying cargo for the USAAF and in early 1943 the Groupement Aerien Mixte No 8 was formed with the remnants of GB 1/25, 11/23 and 1/11, operating in the night bomber role against the Germans. In 1945, 22 of these bombers were recovered in France, and 45 had been mustered in N. Africa. Re-engined with Pratt & Whitneys 1.200 hp engines, at least 30 served after the war with the Armée de l'Air, the last eight serving with GLA 48 in 1956 and this liaison unit relinguished its last aircraft in the autumn of 1957. The picture shows a Leo 451 in Morocco in service with the French on Allied side. **Right:** This Farman F.223.3 four engined transport c/n 2 was just another of the odd types of aircraft incorporated in the Free French AF which continued to serve well into the war. Note again the cross of Lorraine insignia on the fin, the absence of fuselage roundels, and also the absence of Lorraine cross wing roundels, denoting that this picture was probably taken after the round-up of the Vichy air force. **Above:** This North American Mitchell, NKJ 692 on rudders, served in the fast transport and communication role. Note the absence of turrets, and the barely visible Lorraine cross in dark outlined circle on the fuselage. **Far right:** Boston IV of 342 'Lorraine' squadron on the way to the target. Note the squadron badge on the fin. The same badge is carried today on the 'Lorraine's' Mirage F.1 aircraft. The badge carried between cockpit and nose is the one of the Free French AF.

Marrakech in Morocco, later known as the CIB (Centre d'Instruction du Bombardement). The Bloch 174 aircraft of GRII/33 operated from Algerian bases against axis forces in Tunisia until this unit re-equipped with aircraft of American origin and left their faithful Blochs to a training unit which operated them till the end of hostilities. Fighter units too received new equipment. A curious incident happened on November 15th at the airfield at Casablanca, home of GCII/5. A USAAF Colonel, Harold Wills, on a routine inspection of technical matters, discovered the 'Sioux' emblem on some of the remaining Curtiss Hawks. Remembering he had served with the same unit during World War I, he made it his personal effort to obtain re-equipment with more potent material, and this at short notice. Thus on November 21st, 1942 the first Curtiss P-40 'Warhawks' arrived. The formation was then taken over by Cdt Rozanoff, the well-known test pilot. One month later there were 20 P-40s on strength and early in the New Year the Lafayette boys started operations again on the Tunisian front. Operating from Telepte they scored their first hits a few days after their arrival there, two Ju-88s being destroyed. On a dawn patrol over their base two days later, they lost two of theirs. On January 17th, 1943 they received 13 aircraft as reinforcement. This second part of the group was led by

Cdt Stehlin, who was to end his career as Chief of the AA in 1960.

German counter-offensive operations by von Arnim accounted for some withdrawals and losses to the Fw-190, far superior to the Warhawks. With Montgomery's offensive along the Mareth Line, and the fall of Tunis in May, operations came to an end and French air force units were withdrawn for re-equipment. They were next to appear on the Italian front, but in the meantime, a period of consolidation went on. It was during the Tunisian campaign that the former C-in-C of the Armée de l'Air, General Vuillemin, requested the honour of flying on operations again, this with corresponding rank. Permission was granted by General de Gaulle and as a Lt Colonel, Vuillemin was given command of a bomber formation. This symbolic gesture of this great World War I pilot (see volume one) certainly did its share to heal the breach which had once existed between the FAFL and the former Vichy French AF.

Whilst those fighter squadrons operating under RAF command were extremely active with the usual sweeps, rhubarbs and circuses against the Luftwaffe in France and the Low Countries, the 342 'Lorraine' sq inaugurated their long period of bomber operations with a mission on the power station of Rouen on June 12th, 1943. Operating at low or medium level, they were frequent targets for the enemy light flak and the courage displayed by their crews earned them the respect of their RAF comrades.

Back on the other side of the front, in far away Russia, the GC 'Normandie', as it was then known, had started its first operational sortie. Led by a Pe-2 bomber it had arrived at the airfield of Polotniani-Zavod, in central Russia, on March 22nd, 1943. Operating from the onset in co-operation with its sister unit, the 18th Guards (Fighter) Regiment of Colonel Goloubov, the French scored their first two victories on April 5th. Eight days later, three of their pilots were killed in action. By May 7th only ten pilots were left. It was high time a second batch of pilots arrived as reinforcement. Operating from Khationki from

Above: Dressing up in flying kit for mission with GB 'Lorraine' is General Martial Valin, chief of staff of the 'Forces Aeriennes Francaises Libre' or Free French Air Force. **Right:** Pictured in front of his Yak-9 is Commandant Pierre Pouyade, the third CO of the GC 3 'Normandie' who operated on the side of the Russians from March 22nd, 1943 onwards from Polotniani-Zavod, first on the Yak-1. Training started at Ivanovo from December 2nd, 1942 onwards.

June 2nd, they operated during the Orel offensive and the famous battle of Koursk, After a terrible artillery barrage in which the Soviets had a sort of speciality, the 'Normandie' boys and their Russian comrades took off to wipe out the Luftwaffe. From July 12th to 17th many victories were scored but another six pilots were lost, amongst them being their CO, Cdt Tulasne, and Littolff, one of those who had fled to Britain with their Dewoitine 520s, as it seemed now, so long ago.

On July 18th, Cdt Pouyade took over. Only nine pilots were available, amongst them Albert Risso and Marcel Albert. The former had been a night fighter pilot in the RAF and of him it can be said that he passed from 'night to day' as he changed from black-painted Hurricanes to white-painted Yaks. As for Marcel Albert, he finished the war as his country's second 'top scorer'. On August 18th, the faithful ground-crew of the unit left for the Middle East and were definitively replaced by Russian ones, who during the whole war, were found to be most helpful, working under the most severe weather conditions, and with not even the dubious comforts the pilots of the GC 'Normandie' had. They were directed by the then Major Agavelian of the Red Air Force Technical Branch. After having operated from the advanced airfield of Spass-Diemiansk, during several days in August, they finished their first 'campaign' on November 6th, when they took up winter quarters at Toula. It is worthwhile to note that during the previous battle for Ielnia, their home base being too far away from the front line, they carried each day their faithful mechanics in the 'aft cockpit' position, a somewhat uncomfortable place if one knew the Yak fighter.

With new reinforcements arriving, 'Normandie' could muster four 'escadrilles' on May 25th, 1944, and became a fighter regiment according to Soviet air force standards. Operating from Doubrovka, situated between Smolensk and Vitebsk from this period onwards, it took part in the next big offensive in Bielorussia, losing one of their aircraft in the region of Borissov. The rapid advance of the Soviet armies made the Regiment 'Normandie' advance to Mikountani in Lithuania. It was during one of these flights that Lt de Seynes, his aircraft out of control due to enemy action, and carrying his mechanic with him, preferred to stay with him during the crash, with fatal results for both. As related earlier, the 'occasional passenger' of these Yaks had no chance of escaping by parachute from the position in which he was carried. During these operations in the east, the Armée de l'Air was rapidly expanding in the west. On December 1st, 1943 No 326 sq was formed with Spitfire Mk Vcs. It operated at first on the Italian front, where it claimed its first victim, an Fw-190. It later went to Corsica, operating from such well-known places as Ajaccio and Calvi. To the French it was known as GCII/7 'Nice' and amongst its pilots were such old hands as Captain Gauthier, later Chief of the Air Staff on the Armée de l'Air. When, after the Allied landings in Provence (southern France), Capt Gauthier led a formation of 12 Spitfires on a strafing mission in the region of Belfort he was hit by flak and too low to jump, so he crash-landed, his Spit catching fire. Fortunately he had unstrapped himself to jump a few moments earlier, and thus was ejected from the blazing furnace which his Spitfire had become. By sheer coincidence he had crashed on this Alsace part of France, as he had done in December, 1939.

Another two new squadrons were formed on December 1st, 1943.

These were Nos 327 and 328, all on Spitfires (Mk Vb & c originally and later in 1944 with Mk IX).

These formed in fact the first French fighter group which, in company with the Fourth F Gr (three GC on P-47 Thunderbolts, GCII/5, II/3 and I/4) were part of the 1st French Air Corps as at October 14th, 1944. A reconnaissance unit, the well-known GRII/33 'Savoie' operated alongside with Spitfires in the tac/recce role. Part of the original GRII/33 had re-equipped with Lockheed Lightnings (P-38 and F-5) and had continued operations with the 3rd USAAF photo reconnaissance group. While this Lightning unit was still operating from Corsica after the Italian campaign, it lost one of its most distinguished pilots, Cdt Antoine de Saint Exupéry, the well-known writer. This happened on July 30th, 1944 during a mission from Bastia-Poretto to the French mainland.

Meantime, in far away Scotland, still another Spitfire squadron, No 329 was formed, in Ayr on January 5th, 1944. From April onwards, it worked with No 145 Wing, and in addition to bombing escorts with Spitfire IXs, it operated against the so-called 'Noball' targets, the German V-1 bases. During the invasion of Normandy on June 6th, 1944

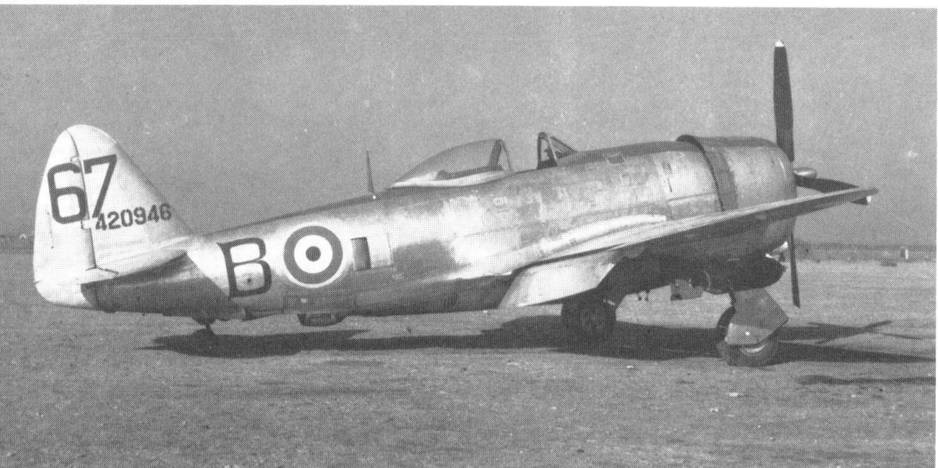

Far left: This Republic Thundertbolt P-47D-25 was one of a large number supplied for Armée de l'Air use. They formed part of the 4e Escadre and amongst this was the famous GC II/5 'La Fayette' previously flying Curtiss Warhawks. Note the special style of code letter with a more artistic than functional touch. **Left:** Formation shot of P-51D/F-6D Mustangs of the GR II/33 'Savoie'. Squadron insignia clearly visible below cockpit. Note size of inner part of roundel on aircraft coded X. **Far left bottom:** Pictured 1944-45 on French soil, this Lockheed F-5G of GR I/33 was part of the (French) 1st Tactical Air Corps formed on November 6th, 1944, and which co-operated with the 1st TAF under American command. **Bottom:** Flying shot of a Lockheed F-5G Lightning of the 33e Escadre de Reconnaissance, reformed on January 1st, 1945 with the I/33 'Belfort' and II/33 'Savoie'.

Below: One of 300 Bell P-63C Kingcobra fighters also supplied to the French who made good use of them, some even operating in Indo-China after WW2, including those with the 'Normandie-Niemen' unit. Note the small fin flash.

Left: This Handley Page Halifax B III coded L8 belonged to the groupe de bombardement 'Tunisie' formed in the UK on June 20th, 1944 at Elvington and known in the RAF as 347 Sqn. Many of its crews came from North Africa where they had been flying before and after the Allied landings there. **Right:** This Handley Page Halifax BVI flying close to the Eiffel Tower in Paris, belonged to the other UK-formed Halifax squadron, the groupe de bombardement 'Guyenne', or 346 Sqn, RAF. It was also formed at Elvington, but a few months earlier than GB 'Tunisie'.

it started operations on advanced landing grounds, moving up via Lille into Belgium in September, taking up base at Wevelgem near Kortrijk, from whence it started dive bombing ops till November 1944, moving then to Antwerpen-Deurne.

Both 340 and 341 sq (Ile de France and Alsace), part of the 145 Wing, had also been on operations since the invasion flying escorts, low level attacks and the like. Via Bernay and Lille, they too took up quarters at Wevelgem and later at Deurne. As for the Bostons of the 'Lorraine' squadron, these had the honour to be one of the units laying the smoke-screens just prior to the Allied landings in the early morning of June 6th. During one of the 'Lorraine' squadron's missions over France, one aircraft was hit over Paris, and rather than risking it crashing on the streets of the capital, its pilot deliberately flew it into the river Seine.

Two heavy bomber squadrons had also been activated with RAF help, No 346 'Guyenne' on May 16th, 1944 and No 347 'Tunisie' on June 20th, both at Elvington, near the ancient town of York. Flying Handley Page Halifax four-engined bombers of the B Mk III and V varieties, they did the usual Bomber Command jobs.

On the other side of the country, and operating under American command, there were six Martin Marauder (B-26)-equipped bomber units (the GBI/19, II/20 and I/22 of the 31st US Bombardment Group and the GBI/32, II/52 and II/63 of the 34th US Bombardment Group). Starting with attacks on railroad bridges and coastal batteries immediately before the landings in southern France, the 34th lost its CO during an attack over the Saint-Mandrier and Toulon harbour. It is told that, picked up from the water by the Germans, he managed to exhort them to surrender their fort to forces of the interior. Later these Marauder-equipped Groupes de Bombardement operated from Lyon-Bron in direct support to the First French Army. In the meantime, some very special air force units had been created in liberated France. These were destined to support the mopping-up of the German strongholds along the Atlantic seaboard.

Left: Of the new equipment supplied by the Americans to the Armée de l'Air after 'Operation Torch' in North Africa were 165 Bell Airacobra P-39s. This P-39Q belongs to GC 11/6, s/n 44-3172 painted the American way by omitting the first character. The unit emblem is painted on the cockpit door, the individual number 9 on nose, and there is no fin or rudder flash. **Centre left:** Line up of Lockheed F-5G Lightnings of the GR 1/33 at Marrakech. Nominal strength of this unit was of 16 aircraft. **Below:** For use in the light communications role many Cessna Bobcats were impressed into French service. This one, bearing s/n 331952, bears white and black identification stripes like those used for the invasion in Europe.

Above: Martin B-26C Marauders formed the nucleus of the newly created bomber formations of the Armée de l'Air in North Africa, after the fall of the Vichy forces. The newly formed 31e Escadre de Bombardement with a nominal strength of 50 Marauders, comprised the GB 1/22, 11/20 and 1/19. They operated on the Italian front, before switching to operations in France, during the Allied landings in Provence. This picture shows bombing up of Marauders. Note nationality flash on the rudder, Lorraine cross, a large sized one, under the cockpit. **Right:** During the occupation of France, the SNCA du Centre started production of Focke Wulf 190 fighters for the Luftwaffe, under the designation NC 900. Frequent sabotage by factory workers made this venture not very successful. When the Armée de l'Air took over some of these later on, continuous teething troubles, results of previous sabotage etc made the Fw-190 alias NC 900 an aircraft with an extremely short career in the French Air Force. Pictured here is one such NC 900 (Fw-190) c/n 24, warming up.

The first of them, known as the 'Groupement Patrie' was in fact formed in North Africa, at Mouzaiaville and comprised Douglas DB7 Bostons and Glenn Martin Marylands as these aircraft were now known. They even had some Douglas A-24 Dauntless dive bombers. Arriving in southern France with the Allied landings, they merged with an FFI (Forces Françaises de l'Intérieur) unit, made up of former Armée de l'Air personnel, aircrew who had joined the resistance, or had been demobilised, etc. This unit was built up thanks to the efforts of the well-known test pilot, Marcel Doret, and equipped with Dewoitine D520s found at Toulouse and later at other bases by the retreating Luftwaffe. On September 4th, 1944 it made its first mission against the Royan bulge the Wehrmacht was forming. As for the bomber formation, this comprised the above-mentioned Groupement 'Patrie', later disbanded on November 1st, 1944 and which had given birth to the GBI/34 'Bearn' with seven Bostons, one Me-110, six Marylands, the sole Bloch 174 operational this side of the Mediterranean, plus a Caudron 'Goëland'. The other bomber element, the Groupement 'Dor' from the name of its CO, had been literally created from scratch during the liberation of southern France. Using all possible Luftwaffe wrecks, or abandoned aircraft, they managed to get—with the help of the SNCASE—no less than eight Junker Ju-88 bombers airworthy. Parts for these Ju-88s came from all over liberated France, propellers from Orange, engines from Bordeaux, Paris, etc. Without the help of the engineering staff and workers of the industry, this would have been a totally impossible job. Incidentally, the workers who had sabotaged these same German aircraft on the production lines, were now busy erasing all traces of it. There was even a Heinkel He-111H on strength. Later this same unit was renamed GBI/31 'Aunis'. There were even Fi-156 'Storchs' which, in company with three Potez 631s, formed a reconnaissance unit, known as the GR 'Perigord'. At least 20 of these Morane Saulnier-built Fieseler Storchs were in service. These Forces Aériennes de l'Atlantic were under the command of General Corniglion-Molinier and, besides the Armée de l'Air units, comprised also newly created Aéronavale formations as well as a photo recce unit with F5A Lightnings from the USAAF and an RAF Mustang unit, 26 sq. The Dewoitine 520-equipped Groupe 'Doret' was later renamed GCII/8 'Saintonge'. At one or other moment there had been 40 of these fighters either found serviceable, rebuilt or made up from parts. The German flak positions all along these Atlantic strongholds were particularly heavy. The Germans even had some He-111s based at the airfield of La Rochelle-Laleu and were regularly supplied by air. Losses were thus great at the end of the year. When GCII/8 re-equipped with Spitfire Mk Vbs in February 1945, its remaining Dewoitine 520s went to the GCB I/18 'Vendee' to augment the dwindling force of A-24 'Dauntless'. As late as March 1945, six brand new Ju-88s 'made in France' joined the GBI/31 'Aunis'.

In the meantime, those units who had joined the FAFL from the beginning, had in turn left England for bases on the Continent shortly after the invasion. Thus, the Groupe Alsace (341 sq) left on July 19th taking up the formation of the Cross of Lorraine to bid farewell to British soil. Shortly afterwards they also bid farewell to their CO, Commandant Martell, who had led them with great success for quite

Left: Commandant Martell was one of the COs of the other famous UK based French Spitfire squadrons, 341 Sqn, better known as the groupe de chasse 'Alsace' once led by Mouchotte. **Right:** Operating with the 3/33 'Perigord' were at least twenty Fieseler Storch Fi-156 made in France by Morane Saulnier under the MS 500/501/502 according to their type of engines. Illustrated are MS 500. **Below:** A lone Heinkel He-111H painted cream all over, served with GB 1/31 'Aunis' and was flown often by Commandant Dor, commanding officer of this unit. **Below right:** Serving against their former masters, are these Junkers Ju-88 of GB 1/31 'Aunis'. Luftwaffe camouflage and Allied 'invasion stripes' are next to the French roundels. The Ju-88s operated against German strongholds along the Atlantic coast, the Gironde estuary, Lorient, St-Nazaire, La Pallice and others. As late as April 8th, 1945, 11 of these Ju-88 were on strength with GB 1/31 who also flew Douglas DB.7s.

Loading a fragmentation bomb underneath the wing of a French Thunderbolt of the 1st French Air Corps.

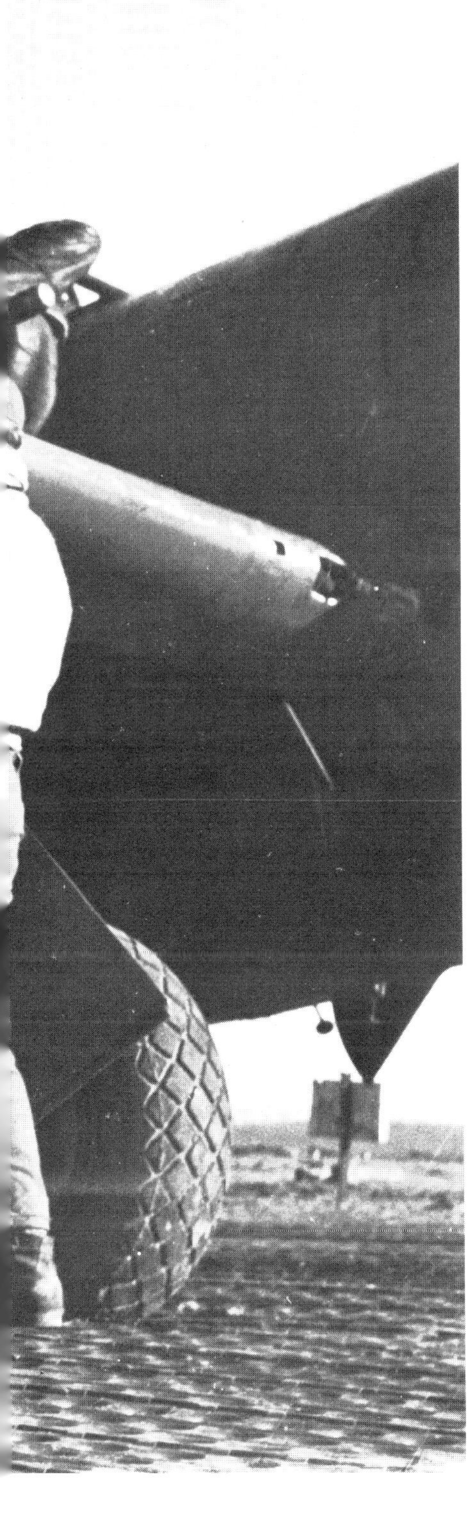

some time. He was succeeded by Commandant Schloesing, another old hand and who had rejoined the squadron after being shot down in February 1943 over occupied France. Badly burnt, he had nevertheless rejoined after the landings in June 1944. Only a few missions were flown under his leadership, as he was shot down north of Rouen by an Fw-190. Another of the 'first gang', Jean Maridor, was also killed whilst flying with 91 sq RAF. Having been a specialist in shooting down the V-1 flying bombs, he had intercepted one this particular day, which was flying rapidly towards London. Approaching with his Spitfire Mk XIV, he had opened fire at extremely close range and, according to the inquiry afterwards, it is supposed that one of his wings was torn off by the explosion.

After a spell of rest in Scotland, the Groupe Alsace, many of its French pilots having already gone to other units, took up operations in the Netherlands, and on April 16th, 1945 it landed for the first time on German soil, at B105 north of Lingen. On April 28th it finished its last operational sortie, on a high-altitude, radar guided bombing mission. Weather conditions were such that they couldn't even see the ground. On the evening of May 4th, they received the news of the German request for armistice.

Not all the French fighter pilots finished the war in the west serving with 'French' squadrons. Some remained with their RAF comrades for personal reasons, whilst others, due to their experience, were to gain important commissions in the RAF. One such was Pierre Clostermann who, at the end of the war, was Wing Commander Flying of No 122 Wing, flying Hawker Tempest Mk Vs and who led his wing for its final mission on May 3rd, 1945. North American B-25 Mitchell bombers had replaced the Boston B Mk IVs in the 'Lorraine' squadron. These Mitchell B Mk IIIs as they were known in the RAF arrived early in April and on May 2nd the French flew their last sortie with them against railway yards at Itzehoe. The Halifax B Mk III-equipped 'Guyenne' squadron bombed the enemy for the last time on April 25th, knocking down gun installations on the island of Wangerooge. As for the boys of the 'Tunisie' squadron, these flew Halifax B Mk VIs at the end of the war. During 13,760 flying hours, both these squadrons had dropped almost 10,000 tons of bombs—a far cry from what their Léo 451s and other aircraft had done five years earlier. Operating under French command but co-operating with both the 7th US and 1st French Armies the Marauder-equipped units did well too. As for the various groups flying P-47 Thunderbolts, they supported the ground troops in the usual manner as did the Spitfires operating for the 21st British army group. The ever-present German flak took a high toll of them and on February 4th, 1945, GCII/5 lost its CO, Commandant Marin la Meslée during one such mission. He had scored 20 victories. On the eastern front the Germans were retreating and on June 23rd, 1944 the Russians started their big offensive towards Poland, and the river Niemen was crossed after heavy German resistance. On this occasion Stalin published a 'Prikaz' (order of the day) whereby all units having taken part in this operation, had the right to bear the name 'Niemen' on on their standards. Thus, by a sheer chance the GC3 'Normandie' became the GC3 'Normandie-Niemen' which sounded well phonetically. Since September 1943, the 'Normandie' had been re-equipped with

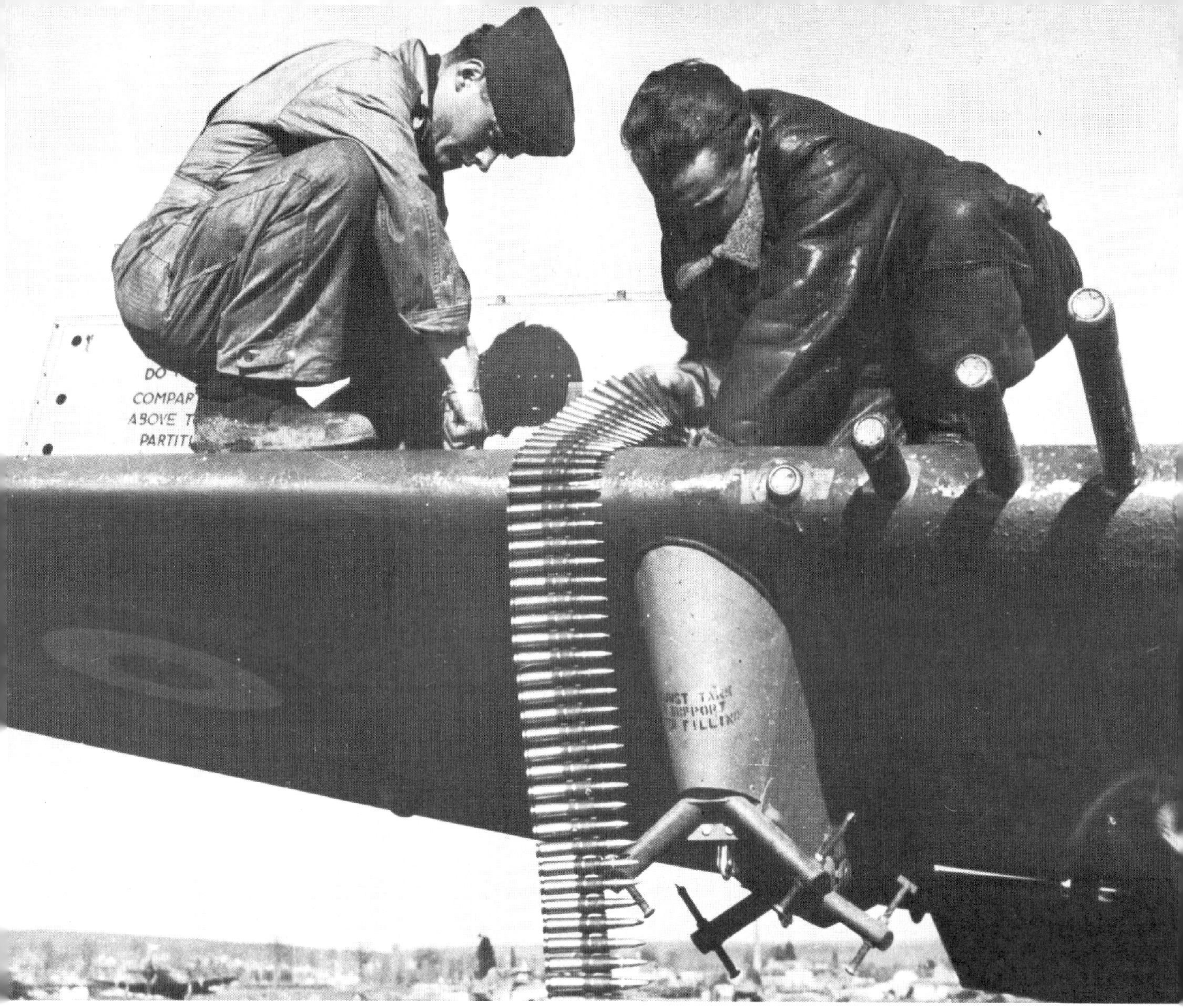

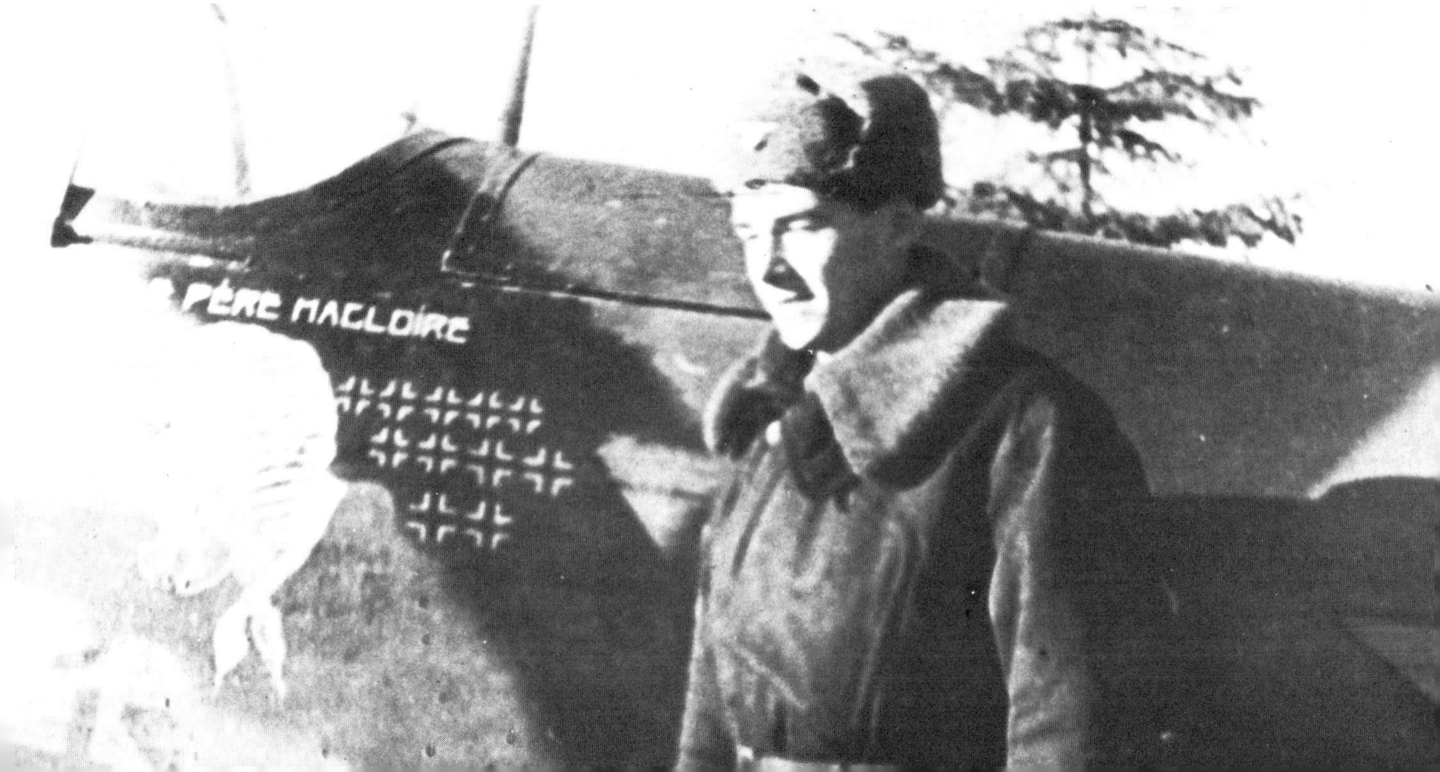

PÈRE MAGLOIRE

Yak-9s which, amongst other things, had a better range than the Yak-1s. It was at the airfield of Alitous on the Niemen that the French changed their aircraft again, and received brand new Yak-3 fighters. Why the Mark number dropped from 9 to 3 is still a mystery which only the Russians could explain, but one thing is certain, the 'Normandie-Niemen' crews liked this new aircraft very much. On December 6th the whole group was presented to General de Gaule in Moscow, and Lt Col Pouyade left for France, being replaced by Commandant Delfino. It was during Lt Col Pouyade's spell of command that a 'unique sort' of fighter pilot was formed. One of the officers, Lt Michel Schick, had come to the unit as interpreter. Just as the other one, Cdt Igor Eichenbaum had performed other duties as well (forward air controller with T-34 tanks, etc), young Schick, with some luck, had been one of the unit's liaison pilots flying U-2 biplanes. When his time to be repatriated to the Middle East had come, his CO left him the choice, either to go on leave, or start training at once with the unit. He chose the latter, of course, and after 'on the spot' training with the Yak-7, he flew with Yak-3s on operational missions till called back as ADC to General Juin in December 1944.

On November 27th the 'Normandie-Niemen' had the honour to be the first French unit to land on German soil, when it arrived at Gross-Kalweitchen. During the extremely heavy battles in East Prussia they lost many of their aircraft, not only to the Fw-190 and other fighters, but also to the dense flak put up everywhere. On 25th February, 1945 they operated from Friedland, a place where once other Frenchmen had fought under Napoleon. On April 10th the 'fortress Koenigsberg' had surrendered. Thirteen new pilots arrived at the end of the month, but on May 9th the war was over, for them and some other new arrivals who should have started training at Toula. Their last base on German soil had been Elbing. On June 11th, 1945, they set course for their homeland, bringing with them their 40 Yak-3s Stalin had offered them. Via Prague and Stuttgart, they overflew France for the first time on June 21st, flying over the Champs-Elysées around 18.15hr and landing at the aerodrome of Paris-Le Bourget at 18.40hr. They were the last of the 'Free French' to land on home soil.

Left: Re-arming a French Thunderbolt for a strafing mission over Germany. **Below left:** Pictured in front of his Yak-9 is Lt Lefebvre one of the aces of 'Normandie-Niemen'. Note the personal insignia, and the name bestowed upon his aircraft, 'Le Pere Magloire', freely translated 'Father Glory'. **Below:** Shown here are Yak-3s, the final mount of the 'Normandie-Niemen' regiment; the second name 'Niemen' was bestowed upon them by order of Stalin for their part in the operations which led to the crossing of the river Niemen. Note the full Soviet-Russian AF insignia, tri-coloured (French Colours) airscrew-spinner and Lorraine cross insignia on the fin.

3 | *Building up a Post-War Air Force*

As soon as the war in Europe came to an end, one of the main tasks of the French air force was its reorganisation. Although some units had been prepared to continue to fight alongside the Allies in the Far East, the capitulation of Japan made this unnecessary. However, the Japanese occupation of Indo-China had brought a period of unrest with it, and it was the government's intention to have both the Chinese and British forces of occupation replaced with French forces. In Germany, the Halifax units were first busy repatriating former French prisoners of war back to their homeland. Others, like the newly-formed 33rd Escadre de Reconnaissance, took part in the occupation of Germany. Stationed at Freiborg (Fribourg) their Mustangs and Lightnings were part of the air element of the French Forces of Occupation. They remained there till 1950.

Still other units, like the GCI/7 and II/7 were hastily despatched to Indo-China with their Spitfire Mk IXs. As the crews arrived at Saigon before their aircraft, they were compelled to start flying in captured Japanese planes. These took the form of 12 Nakajima Ki43 'Hayabusas', better known as 'Oscars', their wartime Allied code name. Also sent to Indo-China was the GTII/15 'Anjou', who formed in company with some crews of the GTI/15 'Tourraine' a mixed transport unit, known as the GMEO (Groupe de Marche en Extrême Orient). From 1946 to 1948 all the Marauder-equipped bomber units were either disbanded, or reformed on transport aircraft. For these a steady flow of Dakotas and home produced AAC 'Toucans' (Junkers Ju-52 under licence) were available. The Yak-3s of the 'Normandie-Niemen' went from Toussus le Noble airfield to a sort of aerobatic unit named the 'Escadrille de Présentation de l'Armée de l'Air'. This unit, EPAA, kept them till it ran out of spares, after which it took over those Dewoitine 520 fighters still available at various establishments. It kept them till September 1953. Incidentally, the Flight Instructors' School (Ecole des Moniteurs) at Tours operated amongst others various D520s, including some converted as two-seat trainers. At least 12 were so modified. The six remaining D520s went later to the Cazaux fighter combat school when the Tours unit disbanded in August 1947.

As for the 'Normandie-Niemen', this left France in March 1947 to re-equip with DH Mosquito VIs at Rabat-Salé in Morocco. In September 1949 it left North Africa for Saigon in Indo-China where, flying Bell P-63 Kingcobras, it started operations from October 30th onwards. When hostilities started on December 19th, 1946 at Haiphong in what is now North Vietnam, the French were in fact engaged in policing

Above: A Yak-3 in service in France in the early post-war period. Note the absence of a fuselage roundel, but the national colours are painted on the rudder and the spinner. **Right:** First fighter of all-French design of the jet era to enter operational service, the Dassault 'Ouragan' reached the first Armée de l'Air units in 1952 and 175 were built for the French air force. Shown is a 2e Escadre de Chasse aircraft from Dijon coded 2-FX, belonging to the escadron 2/2 'Cote d'Or.'

operations, so that this development drained a great part of the air force resources till 1954.

In the meantime, the policy back home was to reduce drastically the number and types of aircraft in service and to standardise on some basic types. The De Havilland Vampire was chosen from amongst the jet fighters available, and training of pilots started at the 'Centre de Transformation sur Avions a Réaction' at Mont de Marsan. First unit to receive training was the 2e Escadre de Chasse at Dijon, whose Republic P-47Ds went to the weekend fliers at Villacoublay and later served in North Africa. Others quickly followed, such as the 3e Escadre at Reims, the 4e Escadre at Luxeuil, etc. Over 180 British-built DH Vampire Mk 5s were delivered, whilst another 247 Sud Aviation (ex-SNCASE) licence built Mistrals with Rolls-Royce Nenen engines later took over in the intercepter role. In the meantime the first successfully designed and built fighter of home design, the Dassault Ouragan had made its first flight at the CEV (Centre d'Essais en Vol) at Bretigny in April 1949, and early in 1951 the first pre-production aircraft were delivered, starting operational service with the following fighter escadres: 2 EC at Dijon and 12 EC at Cambrai, followed by the 4 EC which, incidentally, comprised such famous escadron as the II/4 'Lafayette'. It should be noted here that the name 'Groupe' as used before and during the war was gradually replaced by 'Escadron', as the latter were usually part of the same Escadre at the same base. It will be remembered that at the start of the war the original 'Groupes' had left their parent Escadre to operate independently.

In the meantime, France had joined NATO and from 1951 onwards the 'standard package' of Republic F-84 E/G Thunderjets and Lockheed T-33As were delivered from the USA. It was in fact in the Spring of 1951 that the first F-84E Thunderjets were delivered to the 3rd Escadre at Reims. It was during its period with the Vampires that this unit had formed the first official AA aerobatic team.

Top left: These pre-production Dassault Ouragans, bearing c/n O1, 02 and 03, were the first of a large batch of this French built and designed fighter which remained in service with operational units until 1963 at Cazaux and of which 50 still remained on Armée de l'Air charge in early 1964. **Top right:** Formed at Mont de Marsan on April 1st, 1952, the escadron 1/12 'Cambraisis' of the newly formed 12e Escadre received its first Ouragans at this base moving in July 1953 to Cambrai. Shown here are Ouragans from this unit who formed the official French Aerobatic team in 1953. **Above:** French membership of NATO brought with it the usual MDAP package of

Thunderjets and T-33 aircraft. Shown here is a Republic Thunderjet F-84G freshly delivered and still retaining its USAF 'Buzznumber', FS-823. Note the small French fin flash. Thunderjet delivery started in 1951 and continued through 1952. **Right:** Shown here at Rheims is a Thunderjet coded G-3N of the escadron 1/3 'Navarre'. Note the peculiar style of coding compared with other Thunderjet equipped escadres. The emblem under the cockpit combines the insignia of the SPA 95 and SPA 153, each escadron (RAF squadron) being composed of two escadrilles (RAF flight) taking up the traditional emblems of famous units.

Flying over the Mediterranean are two De Havilland Mosquito P.R.XVIs of the Groupe Mixte de Reconnaissance et de Chasse de Nuit 'Lorraine', the former Boston and Mitchell equipped 342Sq or GB 1/20. Its unit number was 1/31 'Lorraine' and it was reformed at Rabat-Sale in Morocco. S/ns of these French Mossies are RF 984 coded 'G', and RF 973 nearest camera.

Right: This Beechcraft Expediter (UC-45) was one of a batch in service with the GLAM (Groupe de liaisons aeriennes ministerielles), the VIP squadron of the 60e Escadre at Villacoublay. Note the word 'Glam' painted on the fuselage nose. **Centre right:** Interesting picture of a Sud Ouest S.O.30P 'Bretagne', type of aircraft which reached the GLAM in 1952, at least ten being on strength. It carries the 1/60 emblem just below the cockpit and in smaller form on top of the fin, no fuselage roundels and its radio callsign F-WAYJ. Later on fuselage roundels and rudder flash were adopted. C/n of this aircraft is No 8. **Below:** This NC 701 'Martinet' was one of 350 of these communications aircraft built in France by the nationalised aircraft industry. It stemmed from an original Siebel design, the Si 204D, in service for the Luftwaffe. A version with stepped up cockpit was known as the NC 702. Production figure is for the two versions combined. Picture shows an NC 701 on communication duties with escadron 2/12 'Picardie' of the 12th Escadre at Cambrai. Coded 12-XB, note the stylised emblem of a hawk on the fin. **Below far right:** Of the pre-war types ready to take up duty again, were these old Morane Saulnier 315 parasol trainers, some of which were even serving with the École de l'Air at Salon en Provence. Note wing identification stripes.

When the escadron I/12 reached its new base at Cambrai, in July 1953, it had the honour to be the first French acrobatic team on French-made aircraft since the end of the war. As early as 1949 the air staff had decided to build up a night fighter element much in the tradition of the wartime P-631 units. In November of the same year the Moroccan base of Rabat-Salé saw the formation of a mixed reconnaissance and night fighting outfit, equipped with DH Mosquito PR34 and NF30s. Shortly afterwards this Mosquito unit was named the Groupe de Chasse de Nuit I/31 'Lorraine' and on June 1st, 1952 it moved to Tours in France. A batch of seven Gloster Meteor T7s reached Tours in the Summer of 1953, 16 out of 35 AW Meteor NF11s having preceded them. Thus was created the 30e Escadre Mixte d'Instruction et de Chasse de Nuit, made up of three Escadrons (I/30 'Loire'; II/30 'Camargue'; III/30 'Lorraine'). The 'Loire' I/30 was in fact a night fighter OCU.

Reconnaissance had always been the job of the 33e Escadre and this moved with its two escadrons (I/33 'Belfort' and II/33 'Savoie' from occupied Germany to Cognac in May 1950. Two years later it started to re-equip with a special recce version of the Thunderjet. It was also in the course of 1952 that still another Thunderjet unit, the escadron I/11 'Roussillon' formed at Reims the skeleton of the newly created 11e Escadre, which would operate from Luxeuil for several years to come.

From the end of the war onwards, various Escadres de Transport had been formed, mainly on Douglas Dakotas but also with French-built Ju-52s. During the Berlin airlift it was amongst others, Dakotas of the ETII/64 'Maine' who represented the Armée de l'Air in this Allied operation. In Berlin they mostly discharged their loads at the Base Aérienne 165 of Berlin-Tegel. Another, lesser-known transport unit was the 60e Escadre de Liaison, forerunner of the actual GLAM, and who, with two escadrons performed VIP duties and the refresher flying training of staff officers. Amongst its early equipment were such planes as NC-701 (Siebel Martinet), an Avro York, the usual Dakotas and a DC-4 coded F-FAFA, and which had been presented to General de Gaulle by President Truman. The first of several for VIP use, transformed SO Bretagne twin-engined aircraft, joined up in 1952 under the designation SO30P. A good training organisation being the basis of every efficient air arm, it was only natural that the Ecole de l'Air from Salon should operate as soon as possible.

Due to Allied bombing the post-war state was nothing less than a shambles, and everything had to be rebuilt from scratch. Some Morane 315s, Stampe SV4 elementary trainers and the odd Avro Anson, was all they could start with. It was under the leadership of Lt Col de Maricourt that everything started again as in the pre-war days. As was customary, each course received the name of a former member of the air force, who died for his country. Thus the 'Saint-Exupéry' started flying training with the good old pre-war Morane 230, before going on NA Harvards, whilst the 'Thollon' started with Morane 315s. However, the final part of their training was still done in the USA. It was only on December 5th, 1954 that the then Colonel Bigot, commander of the Ecole de l'Air, could inaugurate a modern runway, suitable for future jet operations. Other flying training schools were mostly stationed in North Africa, such as Meknés, Marrakech, etc. The home-built Morane Saulnier Vanneau series of trainers (from the MS471 to 475 according to engine, etc) accounted for over 400 aircraft flying in the advanced training role, whilst large numbers of NA T-6D and T-6G Harvards supplemented them. The SIPA range of trainers, derived from the wartime Arado 396, accounted for 234 machines, the later versions being of all-metal construction. Large numbers of Stampe SV4Cs were also in use in the primary training function. The early 1950s had seen the first flights of several French-designed aircraft which were to make their name all over the world. The prototype Dassault Mystère IV fighter was tested at Melun-Villaroche in September 1952, the first production series of the Nord Noratlas was flown in the Autumn, the second prototype of the Sud Vautour was tested at the CEV (Centre d'Essais en Vol) in September/October 1953, whilst in the same year a pre-production batch of the Fouga Magister jet trainer was well under way.

In the meantime, operations in Indo-China had been going on since 1946 and when on July 27th the cease-fire came into force in this fateful year of 1954, the French air force could look back on some very successful operations it had flown for the army in the field. One of the first of these was operation 'Léa', whose aim had been to drop three airborne battalions in the centre of the Vietminh forces and to capture their 'provisional government'. Drops had to be made at Bac Kan and the neighbouring Cho Moï. The Ju-52 transports brought the paratroopers above their target, whilst others jumped over, and secured the town of Cao-Bang, an important centre controlling the supply run to China. From the very start of the Indo-China war the air force could rely on the services of the Groupe de Transport II/64 'Anjou' which, first stationed in Bengal at Jessore, had moved to Saigon in 1946. Of the other units which took part in the fighting there, GCI/6 'Corse' merits special mention, as it was the only DH Mosquito-equipped unit to do so. During 345 sorties, the Mosquito Mk VI fighter-bombers dropped 80 tons of bombs, fired 82,000 shells and 140,000 bullets. Owing to weather conditions, they were replaced by Spitfire Mx IXs from 1950 onwards, and these gave way later to American aircraft in the form of F6F Hellcats and F8F Bearcats. As it was, the end of 1948—that is a good two years before the start of American aid—showed only 45 transport aircraft on strength, of which 25 were serviceable, 30 observation aircraft of the Morane 500 (Fi-156 Storch) type, out of a total of 50, and 18 Spitfires ready for combat out of a total of 30. Up to mid-1950,

These two Morane Saulnier MS 472 'Vanneau' advanced trainers, were part of a batch of 230 delivered to the post war Armée de l'Air and equipped with a Gnome-Rhone 14M radial engine developing 700 hp. They stemmed from a 1940 design.

Above left: The Dassault MD 311 crew trainer was produced primarily as a navigational and bombing trainer to replace the many foreign aircraft in service just after the war. The prototype of this version flew as early as March 1948, and 39 were delivered from 1951 onwards. This version can be identified by its transparent nose. **Above:** Other British equipment in service at the start of the Indo-China war was the Spitfire F.IX. Amongst the units who operated them was GC 11/4 at Nha-Trang in 1949. About 30 Spitfires were available in 1948. The ones illustrated here operated in October 1950 from Tourane in the Annam region of the then Indo-China. **Above right:** Built in large numbers after the war in France by Morane Saulnier as the 'Criquet', this French version of the Fieseler Storch Fi 156 was known in France as the MS 500, 501 or 502 according to its type of engine, the 502 being easily identified by its Salmson radial engine. Picture showing a Criquet' during take-off at Lai-Ha in Annam. **Left:** Warming up at Nasham are several Ju-52 'Toucan' transports of the Groupe de Transport 2/61. Also seen on the picture are Douglas Dakotas. The picture was taken in 1950. **Right:** Operating from Langson in the Tonkin region are a Ju-52 'Toucan' and Siebel NC 701 'Martinet'. This picture was taken in 1950 before the evacuation of this important town in October 1950.

A Ju-152 (AAC 1, French built) 'Toucan' from GT 2/61 'Franche-Comte' with individual a/c No 88 and coded V (dark roundel on the fin) is heading towards base over rugged country in the Tonkin region.

the front was relatively calm but it became clear that the famous colonial highway No 4 (RC4 stands for Route Coloniale No 4) was to be the future target for the Vietminh, especially as it ran across territory controlled by them, and parallel with the Chinese frontier. During the disastrous evacuation of Cao Bang, and the operations which resulted in the abandoning of Langson, the air force took part, in the first operation dropping relief forces, albeit in vain, over That Ké, and of strafing with its Grumman Hellcats, 48 of which had recently been delivered from the USA. When General de Lattre took over general command, one of his first victories was at Vin-Yen, where Vietminh forces tried for the first time to fight it out in a regular battle. Napalm bombs were used for about the first time in this war. A Morane 500 (Fi-156) flew the general (and also the High Commissioner of France) to the beleaguered fort on January 14th, 1951, and all available air transports flew from all parts of the country to Hanoi with reinforcements.

During incidents in the region of Lai Chau against the Viet regiment No 148 and Chinese regulars, it was again the air force who flew in the Commandos and fusiliers and bombed the enemy out of nearby Phong Tho and Tsin Ho. It was during that year that the 'Normandie-Niemen' Hellcats were split up, one flight at Tourane and the other at Saigon.

In Annam, the air base of Nhatrang was one of the principal air force centres, from whence one of the few Spitfire Mk IX units had operated. It was shortly after the arrival of General de Lattre de Tassigny that the Armée de l'Air received another much wanted type of aircraft for its operations. Lent by the Americans, the first B-26 Invaders arrived at Tan Son Nhut air base near Saigon in November 1950 to train the French crews. Their first B-26-equipped unit, GBI/19 'Gascogne' was formed on January 1st, 1951 at Tourane with 17 Douglas B-26B Invaders and eight of the B-26C variety.

This Groupe de Bombardement had detachments at Saigon, Tourane and Haiphong. Frequently used by the high command for their range and tremendous firepower, one of their best remembered actions of 1951 was during General Salan's 'trap' at Nghia Lo. A basin surrounded

Above: Servicing a B-26B Invader from the Cat-Bi based detachment of GB 1/19. This airbase was close near the important port of Haiphong. Other detachments served at Tourane and Saigon-Than-Son-Nhut. Photograph taken in 1951. **Left:** Standing in front of their B-26B are the navigator (left) and captain (pilot) of an aircraft belonging to GB 1/19.

by mountains, it possessed an aerodrome and had been made a stronghold which Giap wanted to erase with his crack No 312 division. Starting its attack in the usually well prepared way, General Giap rushed his infantry and suicide squads against the French on the night of October 2nd, 1951, at 04.00hr. Around 05.00hr the French positions were suddenly lit up by flares all over the place, while out of the sky fighter-bombers dived upon the Vietminh infantry. Unexpected as this attack had been, they were attacked again around 07.00hr by a large formation of Invaders, followed by napalm-dropping Bearcats. On October 15th, some of the retreating Viets were again attacked by fighters who had been directed to their target by a local partisan unit. Typical of how a well-prepared air support mission could be, it also indicated that even more aircraft were urgently required to give the army some much-needed support. Thus, in early 1952, a former transport unit, whose Dakotas were already in the breach in Indo-China was reformed as GBI/25 'Tunisie' and stationed at Cat-Bi near Haiphong. In the meantime, a small reconnaissance unit (ERB26 for Escadrille de Reconnaissance No 26) received four RB-26C Invaders. Another recce unit, the Erom 80 (Escadrille de Reconnaissance d'Outre Mer No 80 or overseas recce sq) operated alongside it, first with Siebel 'Martinets' and later with F8F-1 Bearcats. During the various operations mounted by the high command such as 'Meknes' and 'Atlas', Ju-52-equipped transport groups operated from Nha Trang in Annam during 1953. GCI/21 'Artois', equipped with Bearcats, operated on missions at Dong Hoi in June of the same year, supporting operation 'Picardie'. Prior to this, the air force had again played an extremely important role in securing the complete supply and logistics of the stronghold of Na San. Situated 190km by air from Hanoi, Na San controlled the only communication road which enabled the Vietminh forces to supply Lai-Chau and Dien Bien Phu by truck or cart from bases in north Annam. An air lift supported all this, some days up to 84 Dakotas landing there. From bulldozers to packmules, food and guns, everything came via the air route. Even civilian transports such as Bristol Freighters took part in the supply. The result was that three enemy divisions were unable to take this stronghold, defended by 12 battalions. When the year 1953 started, the Armée de l'Air could muster the following units in Indo-China: four fighter-bomber groups with 64 aircraft available, two bomber groups with 32 Invaders available, 58 light observation planes, 14 reconnaissance aircraft (Bearcat and Invader), 56 transports of which 40 were Dakotas and the rest Ju-52s, 38 liaison types, such as DHC Beavers and Siebel 'Martinets' and the first eight helicopters, five small Hillers and three Sikorsky S.51s. By the end of the year there were even larger Sikorsky H.19s.

Unfortunately Giap's lesson at Na San had been well learned and when the French started the same building up of forces at Dien Bien Phu, they did not know what lay ahead.

On November 20th, 1953, taking off from Bach Mai and Gia Lam near Hanoi around 08.15hr, 65 Dakotas set course for this jungle-surrounded basin, dropping 3,000 paratroopers between 10.35hr and 11.45hr. On December 15th advanced forces of parachutists made contact with the enemy 7km from base. On March 13th, 1954, the Vietminh artillery opened fire—artillery which the French did not even suspect

BH
20

Previous page: Nord Noratlas belonging to the Ecole de l'Air. It bears this famous flying school's insignia on the front fuselage aft of the cockpit. **Right:** Dassault Mirage IIIRD of the escadron 3/33 "Moselle" during a Royal Flush exercise in Belgium. **Above:** Aérospatiale (Nord) Transall of the 61e Escadre de Transport from Orléans-Bricy. **Above right:** Sud Vautour IIN of the escadron 2/30 "Normandie-Niemen" whose badge is shown on the fin of the aircraft. **Next page, top:** Dassault Mirage IIIC of the CAFDA (Air Defence Command)'s 10e Escadre de Chasse from Creil. **Bottom:** Dassault Mirage IVA of the FAS (Strategic Bomber Force). Aircraft shown belongs to escadron de bombardement 3/93 "Sambre" from Cambrai-Epinoy.

343
30-MR
33-TF
367

Taxiing for another mission is this Invader of GB 1/19 'Gascogne' 434530 'M'.

Above: This Invader flying over the Tonkin delta is of the B-26C sub type, with the glazed bombardier's nose. It belongs to the GB 1/25 'Tunisie' and ended its career in March 1954 when shot down by Viet-Minh anti-aircraft fire. **Centre left:** The Grumman Hellcat not only operated with the Aeronavale, but also with the Armée de l'Air in Indo-China. Seen here is a F6F-5 Hellcat of the GC 11/9 'Auvergne' during a mission flown in 1952. As customary with French Air Force this same unit was renumbered GC 11/21 from October 1953 onwards but retained its traditional name. **Below left:** Starting its take off run is this Grumman F8F-1 Bearcat, coded A from the GC 1/21 'Artois'. This mission was flown in October 1952 from an airbase in the Annam region. **Below right:** Replacing the Hellcat with the Armée de l'Air was its stablemate, the Grumman F8F-1 Bearcat. Shown here is one belonging to the GC 1/21 'Artois' at a base in the Annam region. **Above right:** Taken at Dong-Hoi in June 1953 are these Grumman Bearcats of GC 1/21 'Artois' being readied for a sortie.

G
5172

Napalm bombs are seen falling towards their objective, a small gauge railway marshalling yard in Vietminh held territory. The Bearcats flying this sortie belong to GC 1/21 'Artois'.

Left: Flying towards its target, this Bearcat of GC 1/21 sports rockets and napalm tanks under its wings. **Below:** Ever present on all fronts were the Dakotas of the Armée de l'Air. This one is pictured in August 1953 during the evacuation of Na-San. **Right:** Starting on November 20th, 1953, Operation Castor which resulted in the French occupying the jungle-surrounded Dien Bien Phu. Once a suitable landing ground had been established, every available transport aircraft delivered its load of material to what would be a new fortress. Shown here beside the usual Dakotas is one of several 'impressed' Bristol Freighters. **Below right:** Lined up at the Dien Bien Phu airfield are these Douglas Dakotas. The Dakota in front bears the emblem of GT 2/61 'Franche-Comte'.

could have been brought to such dense jungle. The rest is now part of history. With bombers desperately needed, another 60 B-26s of various sub-types were supplied until July 1954. Being engaged almost every day over beleaguered Dien Bien Phu, the B-26s lost four of their number due to the Vietminh flak. In the early days of the stronghold a section of Bearcats were even stationed there, but soon the airfield came under enemy fire and had to be abandoned. Every possible air support was given and losses rose accordingly, even including navy planes. Piloted by American volunteers, the French even received the support of Fairchild C-119 Flying Boxcars, at least one of which was damaged on the airfield. However, these C-119s did not belong to the Armée de l'Air although they flew with French markings. Still another unit, GBI/91 'Bourgogne' received Invaders before the end. On May 7th the citadel of Dien Bien Phu surrendered after fighting till the bitter end. On July 27th, 1954, the cease fire was signed in Geneva.

Above left: Seen taking off during Operation Camargue in July 1953, in the Annam region, this Hiller H-23B was one of only five such helicopters in service in Indo-China at this period. Only eight helicopters of various types were serving at the start of the year. Note the stretcher cases, the red cross painted on them and the roundel under the fuselage. In the background are Marane 'Criquets'. **Below far left:** When things really started to go wrong in the beleaguered stronghold of Dien Bien Phu, the Americans supplied Fairchild C-119 Packets, which although bearing French air force roundels, were piloted by American volunteers of the Flying Tiger company of General Claire Chennault. Sometimes they were flown by mixed American-French crews. **Above:** As long as the Vietminh artillery did not have the runway under fire, a fighter detachment of Bearcats belonging to GC/22 'Saintonge' was stationed at Dien Bien Phu. Aircraft H, I and M of this unit are identified on this picture. Note the emblem painted just underneath the code letters. **Left:** Probably supplied through US aid, small numbers of De Havilland Canada L-20A Beavers saw operation with the Armée de l'Air in 1953/54. This one belongs to the ELA 53 (Escadrille de Liaison Aérienne) one of the many independent communication squadrons operated overseas. Picture was taken at the Hanoi Bach Mai airbase in March 1954.

With the cessation of hostilities in Indo-China, most of the B-26s were returned to the USA, and the Bearcats were either transferred to the fledgling South Vietnamese AF as were Morane MS500s, or went to Thailand.

The period ranging from 1954 to 1960 saw a considerable change in the equipment of the various Armée de l'Air units and although the Algerian rebellion, which began in November 1954 was to drain a great part of the AA's resources, it would on the other hand be a continuous source of operational experience till the country gained independence in 1962.

Mystère IICs gradually replaced the Ouragan in some of the Escadres de Chasse, like the 10 EC, for example, but this aircraft gave way to the far superior Mystère IVA, which started to equip the 12e Escadre at Cambrai, whose three escadrons were equipped with it by the Autumn of 1955. Other units to follow were the 2e Escadre at Dijon, the 5e Escadre at Orange and the 8e Escadre, moving from Rabat-Salé to Cazaux in France. One of the last units to get this fighter was the 7e Escadre which, re-formed in November 1951 at Sidi-Ahmed in Tunisia on Sud Mistrals, received its Mystère IVAs as late as March 1961, transferring to France in October of the same year and operating from Nancy-Ochey from December 1961 to date.

Above: Two escadres of the Armée de l'Air received the Dassault Mystere II, a hundred and fifty of which entered service. Mystere II of the 10e Escadre de Chasse are shown. **Left:** One of 150 built for the Armee de l'Air, this Dassault Mystere II is seen here in its natural element, the clear blue sky . . . **Below left:** This line up of Dassault Mystere IVAs depicts early production versions, c/n 22 seen in the photo. They are powered with Hispano-Suiza (R.R. licence) Tay turbojets of 6 280lb static thrust as were all first fifty aircraft built. The remaining IVA had the more powerful Verdon. **Right:** Second unit to re-equip with Dassault's Mystere IVA was the 2e Escadre de Chasse at Dijon who received them at the end of 1955. A formation of 2e Escadre Mystere IVAs are seen flying over a forest.

Mystère II
10-LM
113
2-EN
2-EE
2-EA

97

37629
33 TS

In the transport rôle the Noratlas had entered service with the 61e Escadre at Orleans-Bricy, re-equipment of the 62e and 63e Escadre gradually taking place, the 62e Escadre de Transport operating in North Africa, from Alger-Maison Blanche, Blida and Oran until its return to France, at Reims on October 21st, 1963. One transport escadron, the II/62 'Anjou' had preceded it by about a year. The 63e Escadre de Transport had one of its escadrons, the I/63, stationed overseas at Thies in Senegal, and this unit was one of the last to get the Noratlas, while still retaining some Dakotas. The newly-formed 64e Escadre at Le Bourget-Dugny in 1956 had also one escadron, the I/64 'Béarn' equipped with them.

From 1956 onwards the F-84G Thunderjet-equipped formations gradually changed to F-84F Thunderstreaks. Such were the 1e Escadre de Chasse at Saint-Dizier, the 4e EC at Bremgarten, 3e EC at Reims, 9 EC at Metz-Frescaty and 11e EC at Luxeuil. The 33e Escadre de Reconnaissance relinquished in turn its older equipment of US origin to re-equip with the Republic RF-84F Thunderflash. A third escadron, the III/33 'Moselle' had been added to its strength and the complete wing was moved to Lahr in Germany from July 1957 onwards.

Above left: Two hundred and eight Nord 2501 'Noratlas' transport aircraft were ordered for the Armée de l'Air the type reaching squadron service from 1954 onwards. At the end of April of the following year 71 of these had been completed. This flying sequence shows Noratlas c/n 27, without unit codes along the fuselage. One of the first units to have the type on operations was the 61e Escadre de Transport from Orleans-Bricy. **Left:** Many of the French Thunderflashes retained for a long period their natural finish. Shown here taxying is a RF-84F of the 3/33 'Moselle' sporting the familiar red 'paperhorse' badge and wearing full squadron codes, here 33-TS. s/n is 37629. **Above:** The other Republic stablemate, the F-84F Thunderstreak, equipped many of the French escadres or wings. Illustrated is one of the escadron 1/3 'Navarre', s/n 28869. Note the emblem of one of the Navarre's escadrilles just below the rear of the cockpit canopy, the SPA 153 of WWI tradition. The other being the SPA 95 is painted on the other side of the fuselage. **Right:** Doing his pre-flight checks, this pilot belongs to the escadron 2/4 'La Fayette' of the F-84F equipped 4e Escadre de Chasse. The stork emblem seen on this side of the fuselage belongs to the WWI SPA 124.

In March 1960, however, two of the escadrons with the HQ of the 33e Escadre were again on French soil, at the newly-equipped base of Strasbourg-Entzheim, only the III/33 remained in Lahr until July 1961, when it moved back to France at Luxeuil.

In 1956 the first of a large batch of Fouga Magister jet trainers reached the air force training command, and in 1956/57 the Ecole de l'Air at Salon started training with it. It was thus the first air force in the world to start basic flying training on jet types. The Morane Saulnier MS733 'Alcyon', of which 70 had been delivered out of a total of 130, was also used at Salon and other FTS units as either a basic gunnery trainer or for grading flying when enough Fouga Magisters became available. Also in 1956 was formed an important new command, the CAB or Commandement de l'Aviation de Bombardement, which can rightly be considered as the parent organisation from which stemmed the present strategic bomber force. It all started with the first crews intended as flying instructors for this command, taking up a 'bomber course' in Britain on EE (now BAC) Canberras, after which operations started from the CIB (Centre d'Instruction du Bombardement) at Cognac from January 1st, 1957 onwards on B-26 Invaders. From there pilots were sent on jet conversion to Meknes in Morocco on T-33s and Ouragans, coming back to train on the very first Vautour IIB jet bombers which reached the AA in the course of 1957. Later the CIB328 at Bordeaux-Mérignac took over with Douglas B-26 Invaders, Fouga Magisters and Sud Vautour IIBs. These Vautour jet bombers started to equip the 92e Escadre de Bombardement at the same base. Navigators were of course trained first of all on the Dassault Flamant (MD311), after which crews formated on both radar, leader or strafer versions of the B-26. In the meantime at Tours, the CIPN (Centre d'Instruction du Personnel Navigant No 346) had taken over the formation of 'all weather' or night fighter crews, as they were still called, from the escadron I/30 'Loire'. This CIPN346 had a specially equipped version of the Dassault Flamant MD315 with AI Mk 10 radar and gradually received the AW Meteor NF11s and some T7s when the first Sud Vautour IIN night fighters reached the 30e Escadre in March 1957. From February 1961 onwards, the whole wing moved to Reims, including the by then named CITT 346 (Centre d'Instruction Tout Temps) which was the former CIPN346.

Above left: When the first pre-production Fouga Magisters took to the air, they inaugurated a milestone in Armée de l'Air pilot training. A hundred and ninety three comprised the first production order, and the first of these aircraft took the air in February 1956. The same year the École de l'Air at Salon de Provence was the first to operate them. Ideally suited for aerobatics, the school soon formed an acrobatic team, which from 1964 onwards became the new 'Patrouille de France'. Picture shows one of this team's Magisters. Its constructor's number denoted that it belonged to a later production order. **Above:** One hundred and thirty of these Morane Saulnier MS 733 'Alcyon' basic trainers were ordered for the Armée de l'Air following the successful flights of five pre-production machines in September 1951. In the course of 1956 seventy had already been delivered. Photograph shows a formation of MS 733 belonging to the École de l'Air at Salon. **Above right:** From 1951 onwards, Lockheed's versatile T-33A jet trainer was supplied in large quantity through MDAP. This one shown still has its USAF buzz-number, as well as a red painted rear fuselage. **Right:** Sud Aviation's Vautour twin-jet first prototype flew as early as October 1952. Intended to be made in three different versions for the Armée de l'Air, the single seat attack variant was dropped for budgetary and other reasons. The all-weather fighter and bomber versions, both two seat versions, were ordered into production, and seventy of the Vautour IIN night type were built for the French air force. Picture shows brand new Sud Vautours of the IIN and IIB sub types being readied on the flight line.

23
AU

TR-487
117487

Above: The Vautour's peculiar look on the ground is noticeable here. A brand new aircraft c/n 313, its unit codes have not yet been applied. **Left:** Boarding their aircraft, a Vautour IIB, one of the first eleven delivered, are these members of the 92e Escadre at Bordeaux. **Centre right:** This Gloster Meteor T.7 is one of a batch of seven which served with the 30e Escadre Mixte d'Instruction et de Chasse at Tours and later at Rheims when its parent unit was known as the 30e Escadre de Chasse Tout Temps. They arrived in the summer of 1953, later going to the CINP 346, a night fighter OTU also belonging to the 30e Escadre, when the latter got 32 AW Meteor NF IIs to equip its three escadrons. Picture shows a Meteor T.7 coded 346-QW with serial number F.8. **Top right:** This AW Meteor NF II, coded 346-QN with serial number NFII-41 once served with one of the escadrons of the 30e Escadre, who got 32 from ex-RAF stocks in the summer of 1954. The one pictured here belongs to the CITT, forerunner of the present EETT 12.030 (Escadron d'Entrainement Tout Temps). **Right:** Flying in prototype form in March 1955, the Sud Aviation Alouette II, one of the most successful helicopters in the world, was ordered in quantity production for all French services. The Armée de l'Air for her part had 19 of them in Algeria in 1958, 105 of them serving at home or abroad in 1964.

346-QN
346-QW  
XF 
RTER

From 1950 to 1961 the transport liaison units had received the first of Sud Alouette IIs and Sud/Sikorsky H-34 helicopters, Max Holste Broussards were used on various short-range flights and as maids of all work at various stations. Still in service were numbers of Siebel (NC701s) Martinets, Nord 1101 Noralphas (or Ramiers) and Ju-52s (Toucans) which stemmed from original German designs. There were of course the usual Dakotas, Dassault Flamants and even Caudron Goëlands, as well as Beechcraft Expediters. The Glam had received its first DC-6 as well as a mixed flight of helicopters for VIP flights between Villacoublay and the centre of the capital.

Two Armée de l'Air fighter wings, the 3e and 11e Escadre de Chasse, were to be equipped with North American F-100D Super Sabres (and some F-100Fs of the two-seat version). The first to get these was the 11e EC at Luxeuil, who operated them from 1958 onwards, and moved to Bremgarten in Germany in June 1961. The other was the 3e Escadre de Chasse at Reims, who upon arrival of the 30e Escadre from Tours, left for Lahr in Germany. Both these F-100-equipped units were Nato-assigned strike wings with nuclear capability.

If the period 1950-1960 had thus brought a considerable change of equipment to the NATO-assigned units of the Ier CATAC (Corps Aérien Tactique) and the all weather fighter wing of the air defence command, the day intercepter units too received new aircraft. Thus the 12e Escadre de Chasse at Cambrai was the first to get the Dassault Super Mystère B.2. This, France's first supersonic fighter (Mach 1.35) of indigenous design, reached the 12e Escadre in 1958, equipping its two escadrons, the 1/12 'Cambresis' and 2/12 'Cornouaille'. This was followed by the 10e Escadre de Chasse at Creil. The 5e EC at Orange still retained its Mystère IVAs. As for the 2e Escadre at Dijon, this received its first Dassault Mirage IIIC (Mach 2.15) in the Spring of 1961. In the meantime an even more superior version, the Mirage IIIE had made its maiden flight on April 5th, 1961 and a two-seat version of the IIIC, the IIIB, reached the Armée de l'Air in 1962, having made its first flight during October 1959. Another intercepter unit, the 13e

Above left: Shown here in full service markings is this Super Mystere B.2, coded 12-YR, c/n 90, of the escadron 1/12 'Cambresis' of the 12e Escadre de Chasse from Cambrai-Epinoy. This unit received its first SMB2 in 1958. The arrow headed fuselage flash is painted red for this escadron. **Centre left:** Third Air Defence Command (CAFDA) escadre that received SMB2 was the 5e Escadre de Chasse from Orange-Caratat. **Below left:** An escadron line up of Cambrai stationed SMB2 in all their splendour. The aircraft belong to the 2/12 'Cornouaille' and have the fuselage flash and fin rake painted a grass green. Note the bulldog insignia carried by this escadron on the left part of the fin, a scorpion being carried on the right.

2-EE
Mirage III C
2-EP
2-FI
2-L

Escadre at Colmar-Meyenheim belonged to the Nato-assigned C.A.TAC and flew North American F-86K Sabres. Of the less well-known types operated by the French one could certainly name the Breguet 761 Sahara, four of which were part of the 64e Escadre de Transport then stationed at Le Bourget-Dugny.

Whilst all these changes were taking place, consolidating the equipment and organisation of the Armée de l'Air, and also preparing it for its Nato contribution, the North African theatre of operations, and for a short while, even the Middle East, was making its demands upon it. The whole affair had its roots in May 1945 when severe troubles broke out in the region of Sétiffe-Djidjelli. The slaughter of Europeans and the spreading of a revolt compelled the army to ask for air support. Several flights were made to 'show the flag', but on May 19th and 20th, arms had to be used in earnest, and two aircraft even found it necessary to drop bombs.

The first terrorist actions took place in the town of Alger in November 1954. This was also the year the Armée de l'Air was building up its strength to a grand total of 1,400 aircraft. Sud Mistral production had been completed and in Tunisia, at the air base of Sidi-Ahmed, the two escadrons (1/7 'Provence' and 2/7 'Nice') of the 7e Escadre de Chasse were proudly showing 'jet wings' to the local population. When that country started its revolt against France, this unit was one of the first to intervene, together with all the others that were available in that part of

Left: From 1961 onwards, the Armée de l'Air's main intercepter element comprised the first of 95 Dassault Mirage IIIC fighters. The first unit to receive these was the 2e Escadre de Chasse from Dijon-Longvic. This Mirage IIIC illustrated belongs to the famous escadron 1/2 'Cigogne'. **Below left:** This mixed formation of the 2e Escadre taken shortly after they got their Mirage IIIC is made up of aircraft belonging to the three escadrons forming the Dijon wing, hence the various codes sported on their fuselage. **Below:** Twenty-seven Dassault Mirage IIIB dual control version of the fighter, were initially ordered by the Armée de l'Air for conversion training. They formed part of the escadron 2/2 'Côte d'Or' at Dijon, serving as the Mirage OCU but the one illustrated belongs to the escadron 3/2 'Alsace'. Note the squadron emblem sported on the starboard side of the fin.

Above: From 1960 onwards, the escadron 2/6 'Normandie-Niemen' exchanged its Sud Mistrals, for the more potent mount from the same stable, the Sud Vautour IIN who operated them from such bases as Oran-La Sénia till the end of the war in Algeria. It left there in fact some time before in March 1962. This Vautour IIN c/n 306, coded 6-QA, is seen here in company with a Dassault Ouragan from the École de Chasse. **Centre right:** Operating DH Vampires and later Sud Mistrals from the Sidi-Ahmed base since 1951, the GC 1/7 'Provence' saw active duty in North Africa during the policing operations in Tunisia prior to independence, later in Algeria, and also during the brief Franco-Tunisian clash for Bizerta. This bomb-laden Sud Mistral coded 7-CO is seen taxying at Telergma in September 1957. **Below right:** During the early stages of the operations in Algeria, every possible use was made of the aircraft available to support the army in the field. Amongst the types used on ops were these SIPA S.12 of the EALA 3/17 from Djelfa. They were in action mostly in the Bou-Saadaa-and Afleu region. Aircraft with c/n 29 is shown bearing its bombing missions painted just below the front cockpit. Note also the white identification stripes on wings.

Above: When the Algerian rebellion broke out in November 1954 few realised it would gradually develop into a full-scale war. Operating from the start against the FLN forces were Armée de l'Air T-6 equipped units. Most of these independent flights or squadrons were known as EALA for Escadrille d'Appui Léger Aérien or according to the period these letters applied also for Escadrille d'Aviation Léger de l'Armée de l'Air (EALAA then). They were formed and disbanded according to operational requirements of the moment. Many of the pilots belonged to either the reserve, ot where detached from home-based fighter and other units by disbanding the third escadron of an escadre, or simply detaching pilots from the existing escadrons. **Centre left:** Designed for service in rugged regions, the prototype of the Max Holste MH 1521 Broussard first flew on November 17th 1952. A pre-production order of 27 was quickly followed by another 180 later stepped up to over 300. A large number went to the Army aviation, but in late-1958 the air force in Algeria had 37 on strength besides many serving with home based utility flights. Flying here over rugged terrain in Algeria, this MH Broussard carries its aircraft indentification letter 'Z' in a coloured circle, much like that used during the Indo-China campaign. **Below left:** Serving also in Algeria were Morane 'Alcyon' trainers, an example being EALA 7/70 formed on September 1st 1956, who got this type before changing to T-6 Harvards. Note the armament these aircraft could carry.

Africa. At the air base of La Senia near Oran in Algeria, the GC2/6 'Normandie-Niemen', back from operations in the Far East, had been re-equipped with Sud Mistrals also and from 1953 onwards, had in fact formed the nucleus of the 6th fighter wing or 6e Escadre de Chasse, which in turn was made up of an escadron 1/6 'Oranie' and a 2/6 'Normandie-Niemen'. From the onset of the rebellion, it took part in most of the operations, sending detachments to Gafsa in Tunisia and places like Telergma, Bone, Boufarik and Colomb-Bechar in Algeria. A custom during the Algerian operations was that many escadres would send detachments to operate such Coin aircraft like the T-6 Harvard, Morane Alcyon, Sipa, S.12, etc. These units, known as EALA or 'escadrille d'aviation légère d'appui' or local air support squadron, were on continuous operations in support of army raids, or whenever a particular unit seemed in a difficult situation. Their numbering was mostly of a four-figure type, such as the II/72 on T-6 Harvards at Boufarik or the three-figure type such as the 3/73 at Zenata. The 1955 situation growing worse, 1956 could be considered the year the first serious efforts were made for more air support of all kinds. Various Morane Alcyon and Sipa S12 detachments were sent to the other side of the Mediterranean, whilst the 5e EC from Oran despatched not less than 16 of its Mistral jet fighters. Two GT operating Nord Noratlas aircraft were also in action, together with one of the C-47 Dakotas and at least 40 Dassault Flamant and NC701 Martinet twin-engined aircraft. The numbers of T-6 were gradually increased and, with bombs or rocket launchers, these operated against the rebel formations, the countryside (mountainous regions) often taking its toll from unsuspecting pilots. A great burden was also placed on the various helicopter formations. Even the old Republic Thunderbolts, mostly P-47Ds, operated from such bases as Telergma and Boufarik.

As if this conflict was not enough, the Egyptian government's nationalisation of the Suez Canal and the Israeli attack in the Sinai desert prompted the Anglo-French forces to intervene. Some days before, an ultimatum ordered Egyptian and Israeli forces to stay clear of the Suez Canal for ten miles on each side. This happened on October 30th, 1956 and as this was rejected by Egypt (the Israelis accepting it, and their forces not yet within this distance anyway) the operation 'Musketeer' went on from the Anglo-French side. Some days before, however, the Armée de l'Air's assistance to the Israeli air force, the IDF/AF, arrived in the form of Thunderstreaks from the 1e Escadre, flown from France to Lydda, whilst Mystère IVAs from the 2e Escadre from Dijon operated at Haifa. Originally sent there for the protection of Israel's towns, their mission changed to ground support when the campaign started in earnest. From Cyprus, other French air force units such as the F-84F Thunderstreaks from the 3e Escadre operated in direct support of the French and British paratroops who had landed at Port Said, Gamil airfield and Port Fuad. Missions were flown from Akrotiri, whilst Noratlas transports of the 61e and 62e Escadre de Transport operated from Tymbo , also in Cyprus.

It was during one of these operations that a large batch of Egyptian AF bombers of the IL-28 type were destroyed by French Thunderstreaks. The IL-28s had fled to Luxor where they should be safe, or so thought the Egyptians. On November 6th, a cease-fire was imposed and

Left: Operating with the 20e Escadre de Chasse were these Republic Thunderbolts (P-47D). Some of them came from the reserve flying unit near Paris and others from the La Senia (near Oran) based GC 2/6 'Normandie-Niemen'. One of their main bases of operation was Telergma, but detachments were frequently sent elsewhere.
Below left: Even the MD 311 Flamant crew trainers were impressed into operational service in Algeria. Note the rocket launchers under the wings.

Right: Norastlas transports of the 61e Escadre de Transport from Orleans-Bricy are seen waiting at Tymbou before embarking their paras towards Egyptian-held Port Said. **Far right:** Flying over the Sahara desert, this Dassault Flamant MD 315, c/n 70 took part on a recce mission during the Algerian war. **Below:** This RF-84F from the escadron 1/33 Belfor taxies from its Cyprus base at Akrotiri for just another recce sortie during the Suez campaign. Note the identification stripes of black and orange across the fuselage. **Below right:** Very rare bird in Armée de l'Air service was this Hurel Dubois HD 321 very long span, twin-engined multi-purpose aircraft, in service in many numbers with the French National Geographical Institute. This particular aircraft illustrated took part in the Suez operation in 1956. Full invasion marks are painted on its wings. Here it is seen pictured at Bone in 1957, the c/n is repeated as code on the fuselage.

FC
N° 70

if the political result of this operation was nil, it is undeniable that from a purely military point of view, it remained a big success.

In the meantime the Algerian operations had made it imperative to obtain some sort of bombing force like the one previously operated over Indo-China. The American government agreed to supply the everlasting Douglas B-26 Invader in some numbers, 40 of them being delivered by the end of the year. These were of the B-26B, B-26C and RB-26C variety. GBI/91 'Gascogne' was reformed on September 1st, followed by the reconnaissance squadron ERPI/32 'Armagnac', GB2/91 'Guyenne' following in December. Operating from Bone-Les Salines and Oran-La Sénia, they were followed by many others bought directly by the French. Even the 2/6 'Normandie-Niemen' operated them on night operations before it re-equipped with the Sud Vautour IIN in 1960. Due to the particular form of operations, there was a constant, and very urgent demand for medium lift helicopters. The Sikorsky S-55, already in limited service, proved too small, and both the S-58 version (H-34) and the Vertol H-21 were high on the list.

In July the carrier *Dixmude* brought a variety of these three types back from the USA to form the GMH-57 (Groupement Mixte d'Hélicoptères). This was but one of the various new helicopter units operated by the three services. At the beginning of 1958, there were 746 aircraft and 97 helicopters on strength of the Armée de l'Air in North Africa alone. Of these no fewer than 295 were T-6 Harvards, 37 Max Holste Broussards, 32 Noratlas transports and 44 Sikorsky S-58s (H-34). During the year Morane Saulnier MS733 Alcyon armed trainers also operated in Morocco against rebels. Supplementing the T-6 Harvards the Sud Aviation company started the conversion to coin rôle of 135 North American T-28 Trojans, after one such aircraft had been shipped for operational testing in Algeria from July till September 1960. Amongst the multitude of aircraft operating over Algeria were even F-100D Super Sabres which, flown from their base at Reims (3e EC) refuelled on the return journey at Istres.

Above left: From September 1956 onwards, the Douglas B-26 Invader started another career with Armée de l'Air, this time in Algeria. Forty of these re-joined at the end of the year but ultimately there were more than 120. The last was delivered in 1959-1960. Pictured are B-26C Invaders of the GB 1/19 Gascogne on the Bône-Les Salines flight line in 1957. **Above:** These Max Holste Broussards operating from the air base of Telergma belong to the 3/45 squadron. They are of an early production batch, c/n 10 and 16 being in front of the picture. **Far left:** With need for more and more 'coin' aircraft, the French air force started operation trials with a Sud Aviation modified North American T-28 Trojan in Algeria in August–September 1959. Hundred and thirty of these saw service with various EALAs. This one, pictured at Telergma in 1960 belongs to the EALA 03/04. It bears the s/n 52/1206 and the Sud Aviation c/n 6. These T-28 were known as Fennecs in the Armée de l'Air. Note the wing armament. **Left:** During the Algerian war, the French made an extensive use of various types of helicopters and they were in fact pioneers in the way of operating these in the armed role. Half way this campaign, in 1958, they had over forty of the depicted Sikorsky-S-58 (H-34) in service. Later on Sud Aviation took up licenced production of the type for the Armée de l'Air.

42171
3-IS

Second escadre to receive Super Sabres was the 3rd then stationed at Reims. Flying nonstop over the Atlantic, their new mounts arrived in February, 1959 to equip the escadron 1/3 'Navarre' and 2/3 'Champagne'. Pictured at Solenzara in Corsica is this F-100D of the 1/3. During the war in Algeria, these aircraft operated sometimes against the forces of the ALN from Reims. From 1961 the 3e Escadre moved to Lahr in Germany and kept its F-100s till the autumn of 1966, the last leaving in mid-1967.

When the GC2/6 'Normandie-Niemen' changed its rôle from day fighter to all weather operations, via the NF version of the Invader to the Sud Vautour IIN in 1960 it never thought of being 'in the news' again. It was nevertheless to be involved in an incident which aroused some interest in the local and Continental press alike. On the night of December 21st, 1960 the operations controller of the Oran-La Sénia air base noted a suspect blip on his radar screen. Unable to get radio contact on the usual frequencies, only an interception would be able to identify which was which. One of the Vautour IINs of GC2/6 was then quickly sent off to make radar contact and identify the friend or foe. After the radar navigator had in turn made contact on his screen, the controller at Oran stopped guiding the Vautour. When closing in for visual identification, the crew noticed four exhaust flames which appeared to come from a DC-4. This was only known when, after evasive action, the Vautour closed in and with the help of a powerful searchlight, the navigator was able to identify the registration number. A few bursts of canon fire were not enough to make the culprit alter course for Oran.

It was only by creating heavy turbulence around the DC-4 by a close pass at full power, that the French finally managed to bring the DC-4 crew to their senses. With an escort of another two Vautours, he landed at Oran. Identified as a DC-4 of the Lebanese company, Trans Mediterranean Airways, it had been on a flight from Stockholm to the Argentine according to the Swedish government, to Morocco according to the Rabat government. As it proved, its full load of arms was destined for the Algerian rebels. (Today in the rest room of the 'Normandie-Niemen' at Reims one of the most cherished trophies is one of the bazookas found on board this DC-4.)

Left: Maid of all work for the Armée de l'Air in Algeria the Max Holste Broussard is pictured here during a crop-dusting operation in 1962. **Above:** From 1960 until February 1st, 1962 the Escadron de Chasse Tout Temps 2/6 'Normandie-Niemen' saw extensive operations in Algeria. Seen here over typical countryside, is this Vautour IIN coded 6-QA, c/n 306. When back to France in March 1962, the 6e Escadre being disbanded, it was attached to the 30e Escadre de Chasse Tout Temps with HQ at Reims but it operated for a while from Orange. **Above right:** Parades are normal with every air force all over the world. Here members of the escadron 'Normandie-Niemen' from Reims march past. Note the white gloves, the ceremonial dagger worn by officers and the standard of the former 'Regiment Normandie-Niemen' now preserved by the escadron 2/30 of the same name. **Right:** Quite a different uniform is worn by these Commando de l'Air members during a parade past a four-star General. Note their parachute 'wings'.

6-QA

One of the better-known units of the Armée de l'Air during the Algerian war, was the formation known as the 'Commando de l'Air'. Formed in 1956 at the Mourmelon camp in France the first 300 volunteers underwent such a training that only 150 were left 'operational' to start in earnest from Philippeville two months later. At the same period a second commando unit was trained in Reghaïa. Receiving not only the normal training of the airborne troops, but sometimes even a lot more, these air force units quickly established for themselves a reputation second to none. By 1959 there were five of them. Operating mostly with helicopters of the H-34 (S-58) type they were famed for their ambushes laid down for the rebels. These units disappeared with the troublesome period of 1961, shortly before the Algerian war came to an end in July 1962. Disbanded at Bremgarten in Germany the No 50 Commando was the last to go. In 1968, these crack troops reappeared at the Base Aérienne of Nîmes-Courbessac and are now known as the Escadron des Fusiliers-Commandos et d'Intervention (EFCI). They are the sole unit which today keeps up the tradition of the first (pre-war) parachutist units of the French air force. For this reason they are in charge of the Standard of the 'Commandos Parachutistes de l'Air'.

Two other types of formations well known during the war in Algeria were the GSRA (Groupe Saharien de Reconnaissance et d'Appui) which, flying Ju-52 'Toucans', were the last to operate this type. Supplying small posts at the outskirts of the Sahara they had detachments at Mecheria, Tindouf and Timimoun, amongst other places. The other was the 20 Escadre, which at the end of the war was the only air force unit to operate a former US navy aircraft, the AD-4 Skyraider. With their terrible firepower they operated with great success, amongst other places, in the difficult Aures-Nementcha region. Prior to their Skyraiders, this unit had been flying with P-47D Thunderbolts until these veterans became totally worn out.

With peace settling again, the French air force could look forward to a period of consolidation, and of re-equipment. On February 13th, 1960, the first French atomic bomb had exploded at Reggane in the Sahara, and the Mirage IVA s/n 02, the first of the pre-production series, had made its first flight, at Melun Villaroche on October 12th, 1960. On February 20th, 1962, some months before the end of hostilities in Algeria, the decree was issued which gave birth to the Forces Aériennes Stragégiques of FAS. The Vautour IIB bombers of the 92 Escadre were extensively used for training the future Mirage IVA crews, and in the USA 12 Boeing KC-135F tanker aircraft were bought, the first arriving in France in February 1964. Two months later, the first Dassault Mirage IVA entered service and in October the first operational unit on this strategic bomber, the 91e Escadre de Bombardement at Mont de Marsan, was formed. Fifty of these Mirage bombers were ordered, but this was later augmented to 62.

The transport force was regrouped in France, with the exception of one escadron, the ETI/63 which stayed in Senegal. Known as the COTAM, the French transport command could muster no fewer than 176 Norallas tactical transports, 24 Dakotas, four Breguet Saharas, five DC-6Bs, 40 Beechcraft D.18s, eight Sud Bretagnes, two Sud Caravelles, 14 Morane Paris and some helicopters. The other force of helicopters available operated under different commands. By December

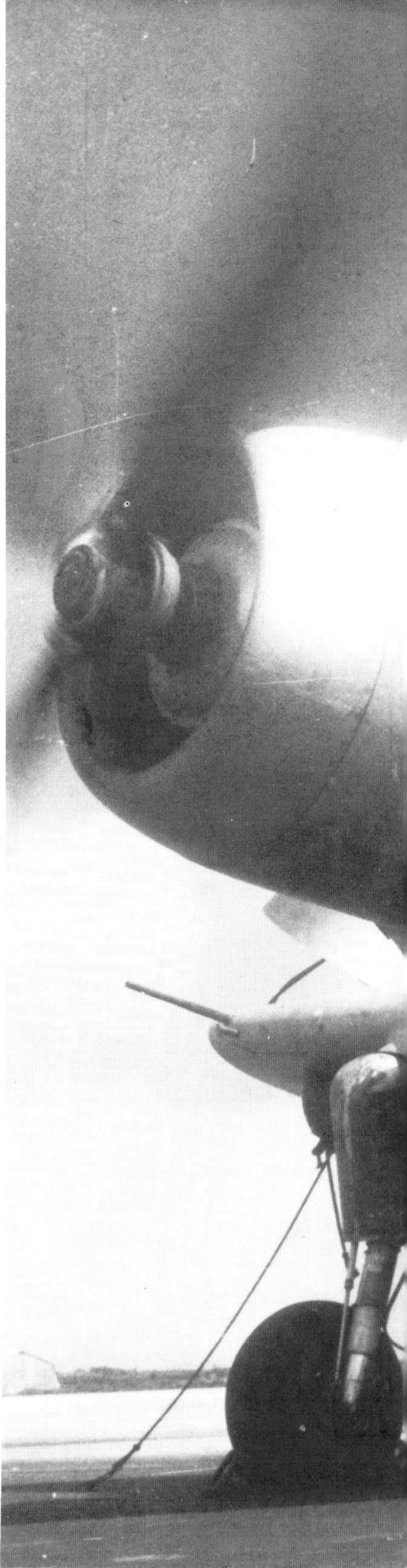

Coded 20-LA this AD-4 was one of over ninety in service in Algeria. A total of 113 of the AD-4N and 4NA being delivered to the AA.

20-OK

312739

Far left: After the end of the combats in Algeria, the remaining Skyraiders went to such places as Djibouti, Afars and Issas territory with the EEA 1/21 and the 1/22 at Fort Lamy (Tchad). **Left:** The first of twelve Boeing C-135F tankers for the FAS was formerly accepted in February 1964. This one is seen during a flight refuelling exercise, s/n of the C-135F is 38472. **Below left:** Part of the FAS strategic bomber force, this Boeing C-135F tanker belongs to the Avord based tanker squadron, one of three such units stationed over the country. **Below:** Taking off with the assistance of Ratog is this Dassault Mirage IVA belonging to the Bordeaux stationed FAS wing, here the CIFAS or bomber OCU. Some of these Mirage IVA are now also equipped with reconnaissance pods.

Above: This Sud Vautour IIB is one of several of the 92e Escadre who completed an eight day tour of Africa in 1962 during a 12,500 miles trip to and from Bordeaux Merignac. It is pictured here at Fort-Lamy in the Tchad republic. **Above right:** Seen here during general maintenance work, is a Nord Noratlas belonging to the escadron 1/63 a transport unit based at Thies in Senegal until its disbandment in January 1965. **Left:** Moving from North Africa to Reims where it was officially stationed from October 2nd, 1963 onwards, the Escadre or Wing HQ and escadron 1/62 had actually been preceded by almost one year by the 2/62 Anjou at Reims. This Noratlas sports the new style of codes and the national colours have been deleted from the rudder as practised gradually since 1967. This Noratlas c/n 91 is seen here during a paradrop exercise.
Right: On the flight line are these Nord Noratlas tactical transports belonging to the 61e Escadre de Transport from Orleans-Bricy.

Vautour IIB

80

Above: Neat formation of Dassault 'Flamant' twin engined trainers from Avord. Large identification letters (here R, U and Y) painted on fin. **Above right:** This EBR Panhard armoured car is seen here unloading from a Breguet Br 761 Sahara of the 64e Escadre de Transport. **Left:** This Beechcraft Super D.18S is one of several which served with the 60e Escadre from Villacoublay. **Right:** From 1958 onward, the 2/64 'Maine' based at Le Bourget-Dugny near Paeis received the first of five Breguet 761 Sahara four engined heavy transports. By 1961 all five were at service there but four of the improved Br 765 were also ordered. Pictured here is one of these with No 504 painted on the nose in front of the unit emblem, and bearing the c/n 4 on fin. The original Br 761, together with ex Air France Br 763 'Deux Ponts' served overseas with the GAM 82.

1895 754
504

1964 the large number of T-28 and T-6-equipped ERALA reserve units had been disbanded for economic reasons and in 1965 the 1e and 9e Escadre on F-84F had been disbanded. The 13e Escadre at Colmar-Meyenheim was the second wing to get the Mirage IIICs, later exchanging them for the improved IIIE version. As early as March 1963 the escadron de reconnaissance 3/33 had started operational conversion on the new Mirage IIIR at Mont de Marsan, coming back to Strasbourg six months later. The 2/33 got its first Mirage IIIR in January 1964 and the other escadron of the 33e Escadre, the 1/33 left Luxeuil and its RF-84Fs in January 1967. In 1968 the 3/33 'Moselle' was the recipient of an improved version of this Mirage, known as the IIIRD.

Other fighter escadres to re-equip in the period 1962-1972 were the 3e Escadre, which had been losing its nuclear capability (Nato) with General de Gaulle's intention to leave the military pact of this organisation. It started re-equipping with the Mirage IIIE in September 1966, becoming fully operational on the type by July 1967, moving from Lahr in Germany to Nancy-Ochey in September. It shared quarters there with the 7e Escadre de Chasse, which incidentally was one of the oldest units still flying the Mystère IVA. This 7e Escadre, old in its equipment, could however be very proud of its achievements as both an air defence unit and as an OCU for fighter pilots. From 1961 to 1971 it had done 100,000 flying hours on the Mystère IVAs, operating from the highest military air base in France, flying in a region with poor weather conditions, even calling their airfield, 'un terrain sinusoïdal et accroche-stratus'. Most readers with some flying experience will understand these words, so I make no apologies for repeating them. Since November 1969 and a memorable flight to Sevilla, the 7e Escadre can also be proud that it never lost an aircraft up to the time of writing in October 1972.

The 4e Escadre at Luxeuil got its Mirage IIIEs in the course of 1966. With the older Mirage units such as the 13e Escadre gradually changing from the Mirage IIIC to the IIIE, and the continuing of production, the 5e Escadre at Orange and the 10e Escadre at Creil gradually changed

Below: This Lockheed RT-33A with codes 33-XU belongs to the instrument flight of the 33e Escadre. Its emblem here is a Lorraine cross on which the three insignias of the escadrons Belfort, Savoie and Moselle, are painted on (in the sequence 'paperhorse' battle-axe and seamew respectively). **Right:** Operating from Luxeuil since July 1961, this RF-84F Thunderflash of the escadron 1/33 'Belfort' bears small size unit code. **Below right:** This unusual photograph depicts a joint formation of a Dassault Mirage IIIR leading a Lockheed RT-33A and Republic RF-84F Thunderflash, all of the escadron 2/33 'Savoie' from the 33e Escadre from Strasbourg. The TR-33A in comparison with the picture below, sports the escadre or wing code painted on the nose, and the escadron emblem on a dark triangle.

33-NA

28722

Flying over the Alps, this RF-84F of the escadron 2/33 'Savoie' clearly displays its squadron emblem just in front of the cockpit.

Above: France's withdrawal from the command structure of NATO did not mean an end to its taking part in defence exercises. Seen are a Mirage IIIR of the escadron 2/33 flying in close formation with a Belgian RF-84F of the 42nd tac recce squadron. **Above right:** Line up of Mirage IIIR of the escadron 2/33. This squadron got its first Mirages in January 1964. The aircraft with c/n 329 bears the code 33-NT. **Top far right:** Re-equipment with the newer Dassault Mirage IIIE started for the 3e Escadre de Chasse since January 1966. With its new mounts it moved to Nancy in September 1967. This Mirage IIIE of the 1/3 'Navarre' clearly shows its Matra missile under the fuselage. **Centre right:** This close up of a Mirage IIIRD, development of the IIIR shows clearly the various cameras used and the way they are serviced and taken out on their trolley. **Centre far right:** One of the fifty Dassault Mirage IIIR delivered to the 33e Escadre de reconnaissance in particular, and the Armée de l'Air in general, this one belongs to the escadron 2/33 'Savoie'. Note the unit codes painted amidst the fuselage. Forty two of these were in service at Strasbourg in 1971. **Below right:** A development of the original recce Mirage, this IIIRD of which 20 were ordered, serves with the escadron 3/33 'Moselle'. Note the codes now painted on forward fuselage, and the a/c construction number painted at the rear fuselage. Rudder striping is still carried on this particular aircraft. **Below far right:** Braking parachute streaming out, this Mirage IIIE of the 3e Escadre is one of 183 in service with the Armée de l'Air and belongs to the escadron 2/3 'Champagne'.

33-NH
JF

Above: Servicing sequence at Luxeuil's 4e Escadre de Chasse, equipped with Mirage IIIE since 1966. These ones belong to the escadron 2/4 'La Fayette' a famed Curtiss Hawk equipped unit of WW2. **Above right:** Sharing the air base of Nancy-Ochey with the 7e escadre's Mystere IVA, this picture of a joint formation of Mirage IIIE from the escadron 1/3 and a Mystere IVA from the escadron 1/7 is just one 'for the book'. **Right:** This Mystere IVA of the 7e Escadre from Nancy-Ochey belongs to the escadron 1/7 'Provence'. Previously stationed in Algeria both escadrons of the 7e Escadre formed up together at Nancy in December 1961. This picture taken much later shows the the old style of coding. **Far right:** This Dassault Mirage IVA strategic bomber c/n 14 belongs to one of the three escadres whose escadrons are spread all over the country in order to prevent the force being wiped out during a single attack.

their older equipment for Mirage IIICs. The Orange-stationed 2/30 'Normandie-Niemen' Vautour IIN escadron having moved to its parent 30e Escadre at Reims in the meantime. As for the Creil-based 10e Escadre, this remains in fact a mixed unit, as one escadron had kept its Super Mystère B.2s.

As late as June 29th, 1972, the Armée de l'Air could show still another 'new type' reaching squadron service. It was in fact during that year's 'Fighter meet' held at Luxeuil that the first of its 50 Mirage M5-Fs were shown in the markings of the 3/13, a newly activated squadron of the 13e Escadre from Colmar. Other new equipment acquired for the Armée de l'Air were two DC-8Fs for the GLAM, the first of which was delivered in January 1966. Three Cessna 411s followed in July to replace the elderly Beechcraft Expediters. Four Dassault Mystère 20s, known overseas as Fan Jet Falcons, were also acquired for the GLAM from October 1966 onwards.

In 1968 the 61e Escadre de Transport stationed at Orleans-Bricy was to start re-equipment with the first of 50 C.160 Transall strategic transports. Its escadron 'Touraine' being the first unit to do so.

Nord 262 Twin Turboprop light transports reached service early in 1969, six being delivered in February, and the actual air force order is for 24.

At the 62e Escadre de Transport at Reims the 1/62 'Vercors' and 2/62 'Anjou' were augmented by a special unit, named the 'Escadrille Breguet' and which received the four existing Breguet 941S Stol transports for evaluation. These aircraft joined early in 1971 and came from the CEAM. This special unit was numbered 3/62. On the lighter side, the air force ordered 28 CAP 10 two-seater aerobatic aircraft for 'pre-selection' flying training at the FTS of Aulnat. They also serve with the acrobatic flight of the Ecole de l'Air at Salon de Provence. Another seven CAP 20 single-seaters serve on the acrobatic formation. Although it was no longer part of NATO's military organisation the French air force has always been invited as a guest to most of the usual NATO annual exercises such as the 'Royal Flush' and 'Tactical Weapons Meet'. Exchange posting of RAF and French pilots was also continued. On the other side of the 'curtain' a great 'first' was the visit made by the Chief of the Air Staff, General d'Armée Aérienne Gabriel Gauthier to the Soviet Union in June 1971. His Caravelle was preceded by eight Mirage IIICs, and two Transall Transport aircraft. It was the first time since World War II that a French formation visited the Soviet Union. During their transit stop in Poland they received a very warm welcome there also.

Besides all the units mentioned, there are still various independent formations who do not belong to the Escadres. Some are stationed in the country, others serve overseas. Typical examples are DPH 5/68 on Sud H-34 helicopters and stationed at Istres. (DPH for Détachement Permanent d'Hélicoptères), the ELA41 (Escadron de Liaison Aérienne 41) at Metz-Frescaty, the EH1/68 'Pyrenees' and EH2/68 'Maurienne', both helicopter units (EH for Escadron d'Hélicoptères) stationed respectively at Pau and Chambery.

At the gunnery range in the Pacific (Tahiti-Hao and Mururoa) the remnants of the I/30 'Loire' fly Sud Vautour IINs, as do the crews of the 92e Escadre during 'nuclear' tests. Also stationed there are the air-

In 1974 the 12e Escadre de Chasse from Cambrai was the only French air force wing still completely equipped with the Dassault Super Mystere B.2. This one is shown with its Sidewinder missiles under the wings.

Above: Photographed during the NATO 'Tiger Meet' held in June 1972 at Cambrai is this gaily painted Super Mystere B.2 c/n 136 with red 'mouth' and yellow and black 'tiger' livery. **Above right:** Stationed at Creil, the IOE Escadre still had one escadron with S.M.B.2 whilst the other had Mirage IIICs on strength, when this picture was taken. **Centre left:** This Sud Vautour IIN belongs to the other Reims-stationed AW unit, the escadron 3/30 'Lorraine'. The complete escadre was scheduled to re-equip with the Dassault Mirage F.I. from 1974 onwards. **Below left:** This specially modified Dassault MD 315 Flamant is one of several as used by the escadron 12/030 'Hautvillers' also belonging to the 30e Escadre at Reims; and used for training all weather fighter crews. Note the squadron emblem just below the cockpit side window. **Right:** these Potez-Fouga Magisters and Lockheed T-33As also belong to the Reims based escadron 12/030. Front Magister is one of the early production batch with c/n 17 whereas the second bears the c/n 326 and is a Super Magister.

10-RW
10-RO
17
30-QE
17

Above: Entering service with the GLAM in July 1963 is this Sud Caravelle III which became the Presidential aircraft frequently used by General de Gaulle and Mr Georges Pompidou. **Above right:** In January 1966 the GLAM acquired an even larger aircraft, a DC-8F, which it kept until 1968. Later on this aircraft, together with two others, were to form the escadron 3/60 'Esterel' of the 60e Escadre de Transport and stationed at Le Bourget-Dugny aerodrome. The emblem of the GLAM is painted below the cockpit as usual. **Centre left:** Clearly showing its graceful lines is this Dassault Mystere 20 of the GLAM. Note the style of tailplane striping at a period when either rudder or fin flash are deleted or painted in mini-size. **Below left:** A Nord 262 of the GAEL from Villacoublay which accounted for five thousand flying hours on this type in September 1970. **Right:** Entering service with the 61e Escadre de Transport at Orleans-Bricy from October 1967 onwards, the Nord (now Aérospatiale) Transall long range transport was ordered in production in France and in Germany. Fifty serve with the Armée de l'Air. Picture was taken during a loading sequence of heavy freight.

Pictured here during exercises held in May 1970 in company with the airborne forces training centre from Pau, are these Transalls of the 61e Escadre de Transport.

118-IH

Above far left: Line up of Transalls from the 61st transport wing with the nose of a Noratlas in front. **Above left:** Air shot of a Noratlas belonging to the 62e Escadre de Transport from Reims. This aircraft bears the c/n 173 and carries no rudder striping. **Centre left:** This Noratlas transport on charge of the CEAM and coded 118-1B bears a peculiar radar nose and serves as a radar test bed for the 'Transall'. **Far left:** This Breguet Br.941 S tactical STOL transport is one of five built. One prototype flew for the first time on June 7th 1961 and four are pre-production aircraft. This one (c/n 3) is seen here during military experiments with the CEAM. **Below:** Line up at Rheims of three of the four Breguet 941 S transports of the escadron 3/62 and bearing the codes of the 62e Escadre de Transport. During night exercises held in June 1972, known as operation 'Saturnie' two of these performed STOL night landings from grassfields. General overhaul at the factory would enable them to reach the 4800 flying hours and the Armée de l'Air is extremely happy with this type.

Above: Tactical transport par excellence but not ordered into quantity production, this Breguet Br. 941 S still with CEAM codes is on its way to the 62e Escadre at Reims. **Above right:** A glider serving at Salon de Provence is the Wassmer WA-30 'Bijave' two seater. Note the schools emblem painted on front fuselage. As late as 1963-64 these were towed by Morane Criquets. **Centre right:** This Wassmer 'Javelot' WA-21 single seat glider is one of several serving with the École de l'Air at Salon. **Centre far right:** This little two-seater built by the Co-opérative des Ateliers Aéronautiques de la région Parisienne at Beynes, and known as the CAP 10, serves in substantial numbers with the Armée del 'Air for initial flying training with the École de Formation Initiale du Personnel Navigant' at Aulnat, and also for aerobatic training at Salon de Provence. **Below right:** In 1967 the Armée de l'Air bought the first batch of twelve SAN D.140R 'Abeille' trainers. These were a development of the well known Jodel 'Mousquetaire'. They were in service with the École de l'Air as glider tugs and other various duties. **Below far right:** Intended as a NATO lightweight fighter in the class of the Fiat G.91, this Breguet Br. 1001 Taon was not chosen for production but served later as an instructional airframe at the École de l'Air and was seen there by the writer in 1963. Years later its bigger brother, the Breguet Jaguar would have its revenge . . . .

XJ
XP
CAP 10  
307-SI
X

Part of the 64e Escadre at Evreux since 1969, is this Douglas DC-6 of the escadron 2/64 Maine.

craft of the GAM 82 (GAM for Groupement Aérien Mixte) which fly DC-6s and four Breguet 765 Saharas, and the GAM 85 with specially equipped DC-7Cs serving at Hao. The 64 Escadre, by the way, moved in 1968 from Le Bourget-Dugny to Evreux, one of its escadrons, the I/64 'Bearn' flying Noratlas transports, the other, the 2/64 'Maine' flying DC-6s and the Br.765 version of the Sahara.

The 'Forces Aériennes Françaises du Sud de l'Océan Indien' stationed at the air base of Ivato operate the GAM 50 on Noratlas and the EAA 2/21 (EAA for Escadron d'Appui Aérien) with AD-4 Skyraiders.

Until recently another such squadron on AD-4s operated in the Tchad Republic on request of the government there. Also on mission there was the DPH 02/67 (Détachement permanent d'Hélicoptères) with Sud H-34s.

The basic organisation of the Armée de l'Air can be stated as follows:

1 Commandement des Ecoles de l'Armée de l'Air with HQ at Villacoublay and directing 16 'Groupements Ecoles' or 'Centres d'Instruction'. These include, among others, the Technical Training School at Rochefort, the Ecole de l'Air at Salon, the equivalent Flying Training School at Aulnat (BFTS) and Cognac both for NCO pilot training, the FTS at Avord for multi-engined training of all ranks.

   The French aerobatic team 'Patrouille de France' on Fouga Super Magisters, and stationed at the Ecole de l'Air. Also included under this command is the Base Aérienne 705 at Tours, which is the Advanced Flying School for 'jets' and has no fewer than 68 Lockheed T-33As and 40 Dassault Mystère IVAs, one Dassault 'Flamant' and one Max Holste 'Broussard' on strength.

   Also under this organisation falls the 8e Escadre de Chasse at Cazaux with Mystère IVAs, and serving as a fighter OTU. Expressed in round figures, this amounts to 16,000 men of whom 6,000 are instructors, 140,000 flying hours a year, and about 470 aircraft.

2 The Commandement des Forces Aériennes Stratégiques (CO.FAS) which has responsibility for the strategic bomber and tanker force, dispersed throughout the country (12 bomber and three tanker escadrons) at bases ranging from Istres to Cambrai, Mont de Marsan to Bordeaux, Creil to Avord. Also under its operational command comes the GMS (Groupement de Missiles Stratégiques) stationed at the Plateau d'Albion in southern France, and operational since 1971.

3 The Commandement Air des Forces de Défense Aérienne. Besides the usual day and all weather interceptors of the command, it has of course the radar surveillance of the country, carried out with either the old 10cm wavebands or the modern 23cm ones, which are better adapted against adverse weather conditions. The Palmier-G tridimensional radar, which will enable simultaneous panoramic detection and altitude measurement, will reinforce the existing Cesar and Strida systems and will work in close co-operation with the CO.FAS at the underground control centre of Taverny near Paris where all information will be automatically analysed.

4 The Force Aérienne Tactique. The FATAC which for operational purposes commands also the 1e Région Aérienne (France being divided into four such regions), is the main tactical command, with strike capability if needed. Besides its own fighter, fighter-bomber and tactical reconnaissance wings it could, if need arose, also have

Left: Main building of the famous École de l'Air at Salon de Provence, known as the 'Piège' to its officer cadets. It is here that the future leaders of the Armée de l'Air are formed, all come out with a university degree in science. Future officer candidates coming from the ranks, and having previous experience in the flying or other branches as NCOs receive their training at the École Militaire de l'Air, stationed at the same base. **Below left:** Passing out parade, and handing over of the flag to a new course, a traditional ceremony held at the Ecole de l'Air at Salon. **Right:** Closely linked with the École de l'Air is the school's aerobatic team, known as the Patrouille de France and flying Potez Fouga Magisters. The aircraft in front bears normal codes on natural metal finish, whereas the formation aircraft do belong to the 'Patrouille de France' and do sport one of the many variations of this unit's colour scheme. **Below: right:** These Super Magisters paint scheme identifies them as belonging to the famous 'Patrouille de France'.

transport and helicopter squadrons on its strength as the air transport command always has such units available for FATAC at short notice.

5 The Commandement du Transport Aérien Militaire. The equivalent of the former RAF Transport Command to name but one example, this command works not only for the air force, but in fact for all the armed forces. It does of course closely co-operate with the airborne troops. Besides its long-range missions it is also responsible for such operations as SAR (Search and Rescue) and has also, when needed, commitments to the civilian authorities. In case of international disasters, such as the recent earthquake in Peru, for example, it is at the disposal of the government for relief flights, etc.

6 Commandement des Transmission de l'Armée de l'Air. Without this command, the air force could simply not operate the way it does.

7 The Génie de l'Air. These can be considered the corps of engineers of the Armée de l'Air.

With new equipment ready to reach the Escadres soon, such as the Mirage F1, of which 105 have been ordered so far, the Sepecat Jaguar and the Alphajet to name a few, the Armée de l'Air can look forward to do honour to the proud motto of its Ecole de l'Air, 'Faire Face'.

Left: Still going strong is this Max Holste Broussard 'maid of all work'. This one belongs to the 12e Escadre de Chasse station flight. **Below left:** Close up of a Sud Vautour IIB bomber. Although no longer the spearhead of the French bombing force, the Vautour still serves in both versions, the bomber included, either with the 92e Escadre on bomber duties in France, and with the special detachment in the Pacific during French nuclear tests. **Below:** Bearing the code 314-ZI, this Dassault Mystere IVA, c/n 39, is one of the fifty R.R. Tay engined ones, and serves with the Jet conversion FTS at Tours, forty being on strength there, together with sixty-eight Lockheed T-33A.

4 | *Postscript*

As most readers will probably know, it takes some time between the period a manuscript is handed over to the publisher, and the time the book is on sale. Since completing my book some inevitable changes have taken place. First of all there was the change of Chief of Staff, with Général d'Armée Aérienne Claude Grigaut taking over command from Général d'Armée Aérienne Gauthier.

Starting his career as a bomber-pilot, he became a test pilot after the war and was OC flying-wing of the CEV, the famous test flying centre of Brétigny. He later went back to bombers as CO of the 92e Brigade de Bombardement, and also took up the post of officer commanding the Ecole de l'Air and Ecole Militaire de l'Air at Salon de Provence. During 1972, the ex-Israeli Mirage M5-J held in storage in France, was introduced into the French air force as M5-F, the first unit to get them being the escadron 3/13 from Colmar.

West of Aden, the Djibouti-based Douglas Skyraiders from the escadron I/21 'Aurès Nementcha' were retired from active service, this unit having accomplished not less than 22,600 flying hours on Skyraiders since its formation on October 1st, 1963. During their last year of operation the six remaining AD-4s of the squadron completed 2,000 flying hours. On January 1st, 1973 the escadron de Chasse 4/11 'Jura' took over with North American F-100D Super Sabres. The home base of the other squadrons of the eleventh escadre is Toul-Rosières, and pilots from there rotate for three months postings to Djibouti. Flight and section commanders as well as the groundstaff serve for much longer periods however.

The former VIP transport unit known as 2/60 Gael (Groupe de Transport et de Liaison Aériennes) became the 65th Escadre on August 1st, 1972 flying Mystère 20, Nord 262 and Morane 760 Paris aircraft. This unit being also committed in the Casevac role.

The air staff decided to acquire fifteen Aéropatiale Puma helicopters, of which two should go to the GLAM as VIP helicopters to supplement the existing Alouette IIIs already serving in this function.

On June 19th, 1973 the first Dassault-Breguet Jaguars were officially handed over to the escadron I/7 'Provence' of the 7e Escadre de Chasse. Previously stationed at Nancy-Ochey where the first Jaguars arrived, the complete wing moved to Saint-Dizier, the escadron 3/7 'Languedoc' keeping its Dassault Mystère IV till progressive re-equipment in December 1973. A third unit, escadron 2/7 should bring the wing's strength to 45 aircraft in the course of 1974. The eleventh escadre from Toul should be next on the list for re-equipment with this type. As the Chief of Staff of the Armée de l'Air himself told members of the Press

At the start not destined for the Armée de l'Air, this Mirage 5 clearly displays the different nose as compared to the Mark III version. It also displays some of the armament it can carry.

779
13-SB.

Above left: Pictured in the cockpit of a Jaguar is Général d'Armée Aeriénne Claude Grigaut, who took over from Gen D'A.A.Gauthier on December 12th, 1972 as Chief of the Air Staff of the Armée de l'Air. The new C-in-C has a total of 5000 flying hours on more than 150 aircraft types both on operational and test flying. **Above:** Canberras served not only in their B.6 version with the Armée de l'Air. This B.A.C. Canberra B.I.8 with French serial 779 serves with the C.E.V. or Flight Test Centre at Bretigny and Istres. **Left:** Clearly showing its different nose-contour in relation to the Mirage IIIC and E, is this Mirage M5-F of the escadron 3/13 from Colmar-Mayenheim. **Right:** Operating from Toul-Rosiéres, this NA Super Sabre F 100D of the 11e Escadre de Chasse from Toul is seen during an in flight refuelling sequence from one of the FAS C-135F tankers. Picture was taken during November–December 1971 exercises held over the Indian Ocean, Djibouti and Madagascar. Aircraft belong here to the escadron 3/11 'Corse'.

Above: Flying with GAEL (Groupe Aerien d'Entrainement et de Liaisons) or escadron 2/60 since 1968 is the Nord 262 turboprop light transport. Ordered for both the navy and air force seventy two of these aircraft had been delivered by the early seventies. **Above right:** Serving for liaison and staff duties this Morane Saulnier MS 760 is the twenty fifth in service with the French air force and belongs to the GAEL or escadron 2/60 stationed at Villacoublay near Paris. **Right:** Pictured here at Nancy-Ochey on May 3rd, 1973 prior to moving to its new base of St. Dizier, is this Jaguar A (for attack) bearing the c/n A6 and belonging to escadron 1/7 'Provence'. Note the insignia of the World War I SPA 77 sported on the starboard side.

25T

7-HB
jaguar

SAUVETAGE

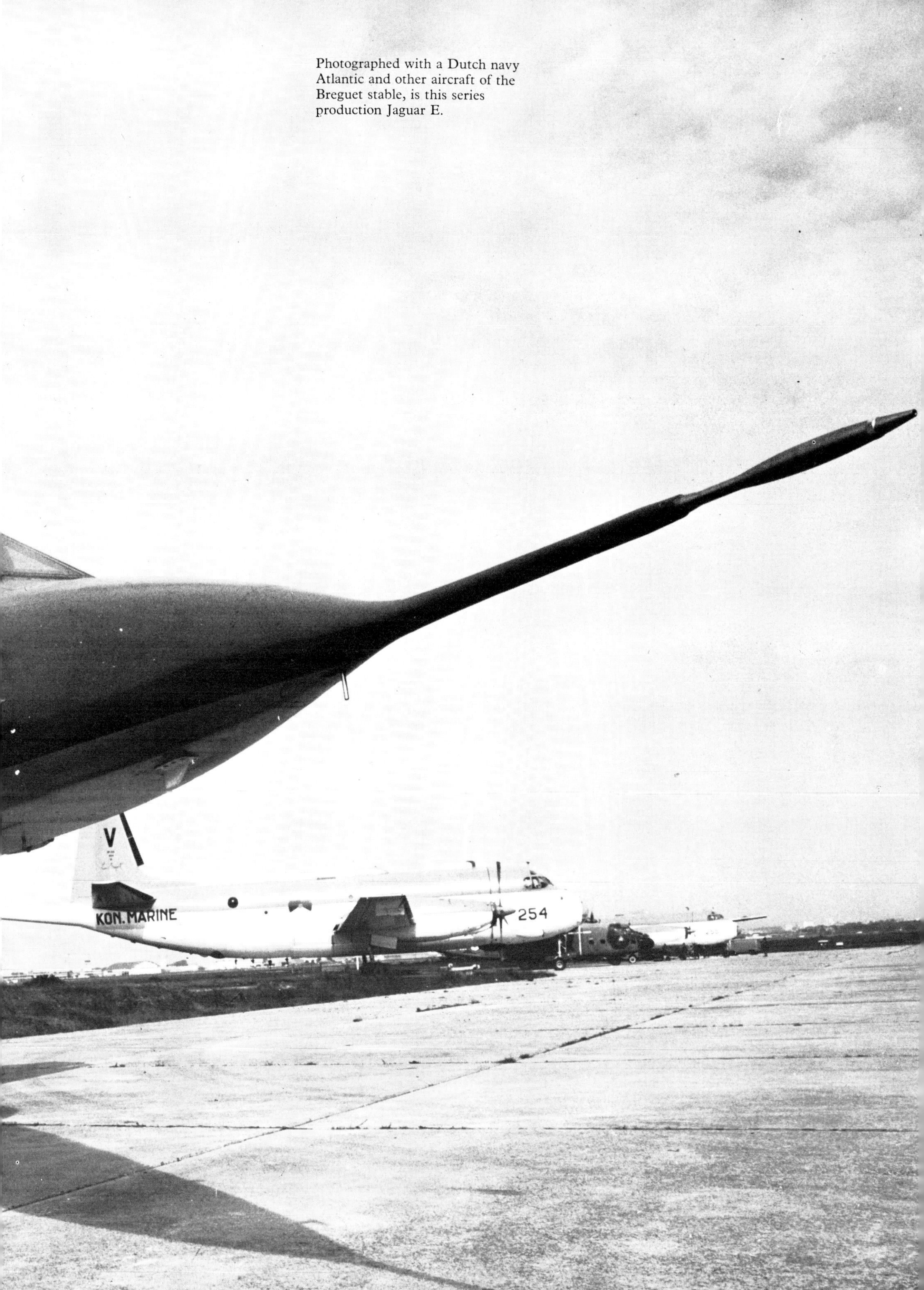

Photographed with a Dutch navy Atlantic and other aircraft of the Breguet stable, is this series production Jaguar E.

during the handing over ceremony: 'this was exactly the aircraft the air force had been waiting for since a long time'. (The AN52 tactical nuclear weapon forms part of this aircraft's weaponry.)

If the Jaguar was intended to replace older types in the strike category, the Dassault Mirage F1 was destined to replace some older types in the pure interceptor role. In the course of April 1973 the first production aircraft arrived at the CEAM test centre of Mont-de-Marsan and the first batch of pilots and groundcrew of the escadron 2/30 'Normandie-Niemen' from Reims went on conversion training in the Autumn at the same base.

The first batch of Mirage F.1s should have reached the 30e Escadre at Reims at the end of 1973. It was expected that the other squadron of the 30e Escadre, the escadron 3/30 'Lorraine' should also have completed conversion on the type by mid-1974. In comparison with other interceptors, Mirage III etc, the F1 has a superior manoeuvrability which will certainly make it a favourite with the pilots who fly it. A greater range and better radar than its predecessor the Mirage III, coupled with new missiles which should equip this aircraft later on, will make it a most potent interceptor.

The Jaguar has been a joint Anglo-French venture, and the Alphajet a joint Franco-German project. The Alphajet is intended to replace the Fouga Magister in the Armée de l'Air inventory, making its first flight on October 26th, 1973, six months prior to schedule, and the third prototype should leave the ground in the course of May 1974.

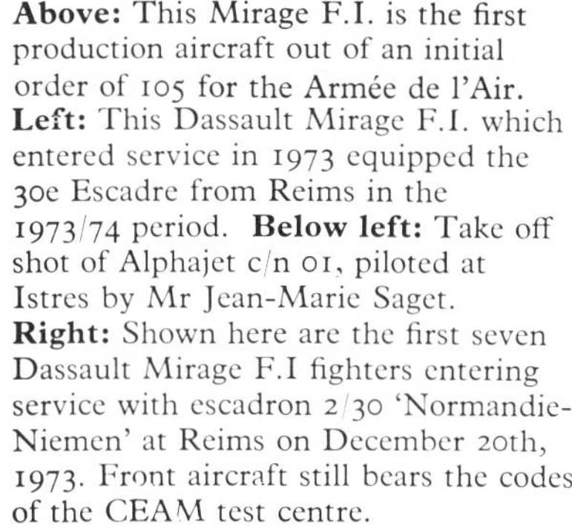

Above: This Mirage F.I. is the first production aircraft out of an initial order of 105 for the Armée de l'Air. **Left:** This Dassault Mirage F.I. which entered service in 1973 equipped the 30e Escadre from Reims in the 1973/74 period. **Below left:** Take off shot of Alphajet c/n 01, piloted at Istres by Mr Jean-Marie Saget. **Right:** Shown here are the first seven Dassault Mirage F.I fighters entering service with escadron 2/30 'Normandie-Niemen' at Reims on December 20th, 1973. Front aircraft still bears the codes of the CEAM test centre.

Left: Mirage F.I (c/n 8, bearing codes and squadron insignia of the escadron 2/30 'Normandie-Niemen'). Vautours of the unit are in the background. **Below:** Line up of the Mirage F.Is of the escadron 2/30. **Right:** Line up of Jaguars of the escadron 1/7 'Provence' with the aircraft bearing the c/n A7 and the insignia of World War I SPA 15 on the port side.

A7
SEPECAT
JAGUAR
A2
SEPECAT
JAGUAR

Appendices

Armée de l'Air 1944-45 | I

Unit	*Type*
GC IV/2 'Ile de France' (340 sq. RAF)	Spitfire Mk IX
GC III/2 'Alsace' (341 sq. RAF)	Spitfire Mk IX
GC II/7 'Nice' (326 sq. RAF)	Spitfire Mk V–Mk IX
GC I/3 'Corse' (327 sq. RAF)	Spitfire Mk V–Mk IX
GC I/7 'Provence' (328 sq. RAF)	Spitfire Mk V–Mk IX
GC I/2 'Cigognes' (329 sq. RAF)	Spitfire Mk IX
GC II/2 'Berry'	Spitfire Mk IX
GCB I/18 'Vendee'	Douglas A-24 'Dauntless' later Dewoitine D.520
GC II/18 'Saintonge'	Dewoitine D.520 and Spitfire Mk Vb
GC II/5 'La Fayette'	P-47D 'Thunderbolt'
GC II/3 'Dauphiné'	P-47D 'Thunderbolt'
GC III/3 'Ardennes'	P-47D 'Thunderbolt'
GC I/4 'Navarre'	P-47D 'Thunderbolt'
GC I/5 'Champagne'	P-39 'Airacobra'–P-47D 'Thunderbolt'
GC III/6 'Roussillon'	P-39 'Airacobra'–P47D 'Thunderbolt'
GC 3 'Normandie-Niemen'	Yak-9, later Yak-3
GR I/33 'Belfort'	F-5G 'Lightning'
GR II/33 'Savoie'	Spitfire Mk IX–F-6C and F-6D 'Mustang'
GR III/33 'Perigord'	Fi-156 'Storch' Potez P.631 Bloch M.B.174 (one)
GB I/20 'Lorraine' (342 sq. RAF)	Boston B.Mk.IV, later Mitchell B.Mk.III
GB II/23 'Guyenne' (346 sq. RAF)	Halifax B.VI
GB I/25 'Tunisie' (347 sq. RAF)	Halifax B.VI
GB I/34 'Bearn'	Douglas DB-7 Glenn Martin 167 Me-110 (one)
GB I/31 'Aunis'	Ju-88A (ex-Luftwaffe and new-built in France) He-111 (one)
GB I/22 'Maroc'	B-26 'Marauder'
GB II/20 'Bretagne'	B-26 'Marauder'
GB I/19 'Gascogne'	B-26 'Marauder'

Unit		Type
GB II/52	'Franche-Comté'	B-26 'Marauder'
GB II/63	'Senegal'	B-26 'Marauder'
GB I/32	'Bourgogne'	B-26 'Marauder'
GT II/15	'Anjou'	C-45 Expediter and B-25 fast transport version
GT	'Artois'	C-47 Dakota
GT	'Picardie'	C-47 Dakota

Armée de l'Air 1960 / 2

Unit	Type	Base
Units of the 1e C.A.TAC and DAT (1st Tactical Air Corps and Air Defence)		
1 EC: escadron		
1/1 'Corse'	F-84F Thunderstreak	St. Dizier
2/1 'Morvan'	F-84F Thunderstreak	
3/1 'Argonne'	F-84F Thunderstreak	
2 EC: escadron		
1/2 'Cigogne'	Mystère IVA	Dijon
2/2 'Côte d'Or'	Mystère IVA	'Longvic'
3/2 'Alsace'	Mystère IVA	
3 EC: escadron		
1/3 'Navarre'	F-100D Super Sabre	Reims
2/3 'Champagne'	F-100D Super Sabre	Champagne
4 EC: escadron		
1/4 'Dauphiné'	F-84F Thunderstreak	Bremgarten
2/4 'La Fayette'	F-84F Thunderstreak	(Germany)
5 EC: escadron		
1/5 'Vendée'	Super Mystère B.2	Orange
2/5 'Ile de France'	Super Mystère B.2	'Caritat'
6 EC: escadron		
1/6 'Oranie'	Sud Mistral	Telergma-Boufarik, Bone and detachments all over Algeria
2/6 'Normandie-Niemen'	Sud Vautour IIN	
7 EC: escadron		
1/7 'Provence'	Sud Mistral	Sidi-Ahmed (Tunisia), later Telergma (Algeria)
2/7 'Nice'	Sud Mistral	

Unit	*Type*	*Base*
8 EC: escadron		
1/8 'Saintonge'	Sud Mistral–Mystère IVA	Rabat-Salé (Morocco)
2/8 'Languedoc'	Sud Mistral–Mystère IVA	later to Oran-La Sénia (Algeria)
9 EC: escadron		
1/9 'Limousin'	F-84F Thunderstreak	Metz
2/9 'Auvergne'	F-84F Thunderstreak	'Frescaty'
10 EC: escadron		
1/10 'Valois'	Super Mystère B.2	Creil
2/10 'Seine'	Super Mystère B.2	
11 EC: escadron		
1/11 'Roussillon'	F-100D Super Sabre	Luxeuil
2/11 'Vosges'	F-100D Super Sabre	
12 EC: escadron		
1/12 'Cambrésis'	Super Mystère B.2	Cambrai
2/12 'Cornouaille'	Super Mystère B.2	'Epinoy'
13 EC: escadron		
1/13 'Artois'	F-86K Sabre	Colmar
2/13 'Alpes'	F-86K Sabre	'Meyenheim'
30 ECTT: escadron		
1/30 'Loire'	Sud Vautour IIN	Tours
3/30 'Lorraine'	Sud Vautour IIN	
33 ER: escadron		
1/33 'Belfort'	RF-84F Thunderflash	Lahr (Germany)
2/33 'Savoie'	RF-84F Thunderflash	Strasbourg-Entzheim
3/33 'Moselle'	RF-84F Thunderflash	Strasbourg-Entzheim

Units of the Commandement de l'Aviation de Bombardement (Bomber Command)

91 EB: escadron		
1/91 'Gascogne'	B-26 Invader	Bone les Salines (Algeria) and Setiffe
2/91 'Guyenne'	B-26 Invader	
92 EB: escadron		
1/92 'Bourgogne'	Sud Vautour IIB	Bordeaux
2/92 'Aquitaine'	Sud Vautour IIB	'Merignac'
CIB 328 (Bomber OCU)	B-26 Invader Sud Vautour IIB Fouga Magister	Bordeaux 'Merignac'

Units of the CO.TAM (Air Transport Command)

60 ET: escadron		
1/60 'GLAM'	S.O.30P Bretagne Beechcraft UC-45 DC-6	Villacoublay
2/60 'GAEL'	Douglas C-47 Dakota C-45 Expediter	

Unit	Type	Base
61 ET: escadron		
1/61 'Touraine'	Nord 2501 Noratlas	Orleans
2/61 'Franche Comté'	Nord 2501 Noratlas	'Bricy'
3/61 'Poitou'	Nord 2501 Noratlas	
62 ET: escadron		
1/62 'Algérie'	Nord 2501 Noratlas	Alger 'Maison Blanche'
2/62 'Anjou'	Nord 2501 Noratlas	Blida
3/62 'Sahara'	Nord 2501 Noratlas and C-47 Dakota	Alger 'Maison Blanche' and Oran 'La Sénia'

Its different escadrons operated in fact independently as part not of a 62 Escadre but of the S/GMMTA till December 1st, 1961.

Unit	Type	Base
63 ET: escadron		
1/63 'Bretagne'	Nord 2501 Noratlas	Thiès (Senegal)
2/63 'Bigorre'	C-47 Dakota	Pau
64 ET: escadron		
1/64 'Béarn'	Nord 2501 Noratlas	Le Bourget
2/64 'Maine'	Breguet Sahara	'Dugny'
EITA 341 (Escadrille d'Instruction des Troupes Aéroportées)—airborne training sq.—	Nord 2501 Noratlas C-47 Dakota	Pau
CIET—Transport OCU—	Nord 2501 Noratlas	Toulouse 'Francazal'

Armée de l'Air—other units 1960 onwards

Groupe de Liaison et Sauvetage No 45: Boufarik
Groupe de Liaison Aérien No 48: Dakar (Senegal)
Groupe de Liaison Aérien No 49: Brazaville (République du Congo)
ER 32: Douglas RB-26 Invader
CEAM (Centre d'Expériences Aériennes Militaires): Mont de Marsan all new types entering service
CEV (Centre d'Essais en Vol): Bretigny Gloster Meteor T.7, A.W. Meteor NF.11, Morane 'Criquet', Douglas B-26 Invader, Morane 'Paris'
ERALA (Escadrilles Régionales d'Aviation Légère d'Appui)
No 35 Sud Fennec (ex-NA T-28 Trojan)
No 36 Sud Fennec
No 37 Sud Fennec and T-6G Harvard
No 38 Sud Fennec
No 39 Sud Fennec
Most of them had also Harvards on strength. All were disbanded in December 1964.

Ecole de l'Air: Salon en Provence: Fouga Magister, C-47 Dakota (two), GAMD Flamant (four), Morane Criquet (four) as glider tugs, Mystère IVA
Base Ecole B.E.709: Cognac T6-G Harvard but since mid-1965 only with Fouga Magister

Ecole de Transition Réacteur: Orange Fouga Magister (will be disbanded when Cognac has full complement of Magisters)

Ecole de Chasse 'Martel': Tours Lockheed T-33 (55), Mystère IVA (40). Was formerly at Meknès in Morocco.

EE 54 (Escadre Electronique): Noratlas (radar counter measures, etc.) One Noratlas being genuine transport aircraft, all others transformed.

Other independent units in service in the Algerian Theatre of Operations

Unit	*Type*	*Base*
22 EH (Escadre d'Hélicoptères)	Sud and Sikorsky H-34	Oran-La Sénia
23 EH	Sud and Sikorsky H-34	Telergma and Reghaïa
20 Escadre 1/20	AD-4 Skyraider	Telergma and
2/20	AD-4 Skyraider	detachments
3/20	AD-4 Skyraider	elsewhere
ER 1/32 'Armagnac'	RB-26C Invader	Bône les Salines and Sétiffe
ECN 1/71	B-26N Invader	Tebessa
GSRA 76 'Tindouf'	AACI 'Toucan' (lic. Ju-52)	Detachments at Colomb-Béchar Oran-Tindouf-Mecheria-Timimoun

Besides these units were large numbers of T-6G Harvard, Morane Alcyon, Max Holste Broussard, Sipa S.12, Dassault Flamant-equipped units, most of them of the EALA type (Escadrilles Aériennes Légères d'Appui) and GOM (Groupement d'Observation Mixte).

Armée de l'Air 1974 / 3

Units of the FATAC (Tactical Air Force) and CAFDA (Air Defence Command)

EC *for Escadre de Chasse*
ECTT *for Escadre de Chasse Tout Temps*
ER *for Escadre de Reconnaissance*

Unit	*Type*	*Base*
2 EC: escadron		
1/2 'Cigogne'	Mirage IIIE	Dijon
2/2 'Côte d'Or'	Mirage IIIB and BE	'Longvic'
3/2 'Alsace'	Mirage IIIE	

Unit	Type	Base
3 EC: escadron		
1/3 'Navarre'	Mirage IIIE	Nancy
2/3 'Champagne'	Mirage IIIE	'Ochey'
4 EC: escadron		
1/4 'Dauphiné'	Mirage IIIE	Luxeuil
2/4 'La Fayette'	Mirage IIIE	
5 EC: escadron		
1/5 'Vendée'	Mirage IIIC	Orange
2/5 'Ile de France'	Mirage IIIC	'Caritat'
7 EC: escadron		
1/7 'Provence'	Breguet Jaguar	Saint Dizier
3/7 'Languedoc'	Breguet Jaguar	
8 EC: escadron		
1/8 'Saintonge'	Mystère IVA	Cazaux
2/8 'Nice'	Mystère IVA	
10 EC: escadron		
1/10 'Valois'	Mirage IIIC	Creil
2/10 'Seine'	Mirage IIIC & S.M.B.2	
11 EC: escadron		
1/11 'Roussillon'	F-100D Super Sabre	Toul
2/11 'Vosges'	F-100D Super Sabre	'Rosières'
3/11 'Corse'	F-100D Super Sabre	
4/11 „ Jura	„ „	Also overseas detachments to Djibouti
12 EC: escadron		
1/12 'Cambrésis'	Super Mystère B.2	Cambrai
2/12 'Cornouaille'	Super Mystère B.2	'Epinoy'
13 EC: escadron		
1/13 'Artois'	Mirage IIIE	Colmar
2/13 'Alpes'	Mirage IIIE	'Meyenheim'
3/13 Auvergne	Mirage 5F	
30 ECTT: escadron		
2/30 'Normandie-Niemen'	Dassault Mirage F.1	Reims
3/30 'Lorraine'	Dassault Mirage F.1	
33 ER: escadron		
1/33 'Belfort'	Mirage IIIR and	Strasbourg
2/33 'Savoie'	IIIRD	'Entzheim'
3/33 'Moselle'		

Note: The 8 Escadre de Chasse serves in a dual role, also having commitments towards the CEAA (Training Command) as fighter OTU.

Units of the COTAM (Air Transport Command)

ET *for Escadre de Transport*

Unit	Type	Base
60.ET 2/60 (GAEL)	M.S. Paris Alouette II Nord 262	Villacoublay
3/60 'Estérel'	DC-8	Le Bourget

Unit	Type	Base
61 ET: escadron		
1/61 'Touraine'	Transall	Orleans
2/61 'Franche Comté'	Transall	'Bricy'
3/61 'Poitou'	Transall	
62 ET: escadron		
1/62 'Vercors'	Noratlas	Reims
2/62 'Anjou'	Noratlas	'Champagne'
3/62	Breguet 941S	
63 ET: escadron		
2/63 'Bigorre'	Noratlas	Pau
64 ET: escadron		
1/64 'Béarn'	Noratlas	Evreux
2/64 'Maine'	DC-6	'Fauville'
65ET: 1/65 GLAM	Puma	
	Caravelle III	Villacoublay
	Mystère 20	
	Cessna 411	
	Alouette III	
CIET (Transport OCU)	Noratlas	Toulouse 'Francazal'
EH 1/68 'Pyrénées'	Sud H-34 Alouette II & III	Cazaux
EH 2/68 'Maurienne'	Alouette II & III	Chambery
EH 3/67 'Parisis'	„ „	Villacoublay
EH 2/67 'Valmy'	„ „	Metz

Units of the COFAS (Strategic Bomber Force)

Unit	Type	Base
CIFAS (Strategic Bomber OCU)	Mirage IVA	Bordeaux Mérignac
91 Escadre de Bombardement		
Escadron 1/91 'Gascogne'	Mirage IVA	Mont de Marsan
„ 2/91 'Bretagne'	Mirage IVA	Mont de Marsan
„ 3/91 'Beauvaisis'	Mirage IVA	Creil
Escadron de ravitaillement en vol 4/91' 'Landes'	Boeing C-135F	Mont de Marsan
92 Escadre de Bombardement		
Escadron 1/92 'Bourgogne'	Vautour IIB	Bordeaux Mérignac
„ 2/92 'Aquitaine'	Vautour IIB	Bordeaux Mérignac

(This unit is both an OTU for the COFAS but serves also in the electronics countermeasure and other roles for the FATAC.)

Unit	Type	Base
93 Escadre de Bombardement		
Escadron 1/93 'Guyenne'	Mirage IVA	Istres
„ 2/93 'Cévennes'	Mirage IVA	Orange
„ 3/93 'Sambre'	Mirage IVA	Cambrai
„ 4/93 'Aunis'	Boeing C-I35F	Istres

Unit	Type	Base
94 Escadre de Bombardement		
Escadron 1/94 'Bourbonnais'	Mirage IVA	Avord
,, 2/94 'Marne'	Mirage IVA	Saint Dizier
,, 3/94 'Arbois'	Mirage IVA	Luxeuil
,, 4/94 'Sologne'	Boeing C-135F	Avord

Some Mirage IIIB are also on strength for continuity training.

Flying units of the Commandement des Ecoles de l'Armée de l'Air including the French air force academy, known the world over as the 'Ecole de l'Air'.

Aulnat EFTS (for NCO pilots) Fouga Magister—prior to this initial flying on CAP10

Cognac FTS (for NCO pilots) Fouga Magister

Ecole de l'Air (for direct entry officer pilots) Fouga Magister

Avord FTS (for twin-engined conversion) Dassault Flamant MD. 312

Tours FTS (advanced training) Lockheed T-33A and Mystère IVA

Independent Overseas Units

Unit	Type	Base
GAM82 (Groupement Aérien Mixte	Breguet Sahara & Noratlas	Tahiti-Hao & Faaa
GAM85	DC-7C (ECM research)	
with also the escadron de marche 00.085 perpetuating the traditions of the 1/30 'Loire'	Vautour IIB & N	Hao
GAMOM 88	Noratlas & Alouette II	Djibouti (Indian Ocean)
EL 1/22		
(Escadrille Légère d'Appui)	AD-4 Skyraider	Fort Lamy (Central Africa)
Gradually to be phased out in 1974		
GAMOM50	Noratlas	Sainte Clotilde
ET 58		
(escadrille de transport)	Noratlas	Point à Pitre
GMT59	Noratlas	N'Djamena
(Groupe Mixte de Transport).		

Photo Credits

Base Aerienne 702 Avord, photo section: 12BT
B.A. Reims photo section: 65B, 78, 105C, 147T, 147B, 148T
B.A. 123 Orleans photo section: 127B
42 sq Belgian A.F.: 134T
Brequet Aviation press section: 129T, 149B, 162
Avions Marcel Dassault press section: 5, 76T, 98C, 137B, 157, 164C, 165T
Dassault-Breguet: 164B
Willy Deleenheer: 149C
ECA (Etablissement Cinematographique et Photographique des Armées): 9, 10, 12, 23, 39, 47T, 48, 50, 51, 53T, 53B, 54T, 55, 56T, 56C, 57, 58T, 58C, 59, 60, 61, 62C, 63C, 64T, 65C, 66T, 68T, 68B, 72B, 75T, 75B, 76C, 77B, 84B, 84TR, 85T, 85B, 86, 87T, 87B, 89, 90B, 91T, 91B, 92, 94T, 95T, 95B, 96T, 96B, 97T, 99B, 105B, 110C, 110B, 111T, 114T, 114B, 115T, 115B, 116TR, 117T, 120B, 123, 125B, 134C
Ile Escadre photo section: 159B
12e Escadre Cambrai: 80B, 107T, 139, 140T, 155T
30e Escadre Reims photo section: 120TR
33e Escadre photo section: 62TR, 63B, 121T, 131T, 132, 134B, 135C
62e Escadre Reims photo section: 126B
Fatac Ie R.A.: 158B
Jean Marie Guhl: 161B
Ie F.A. Tac Press section: 101T, 135B, 136B, 137T
Imperial War Museum: 64B
J. Mutin: 90C, 97B
Jean Noel: 7, 19, 25, 43, 44T, 44B, 47B, 54C, 58TR, 66B, 73B
Stephen Peltz: 155B, 159T
Mr Petitjean: 64C, 81B
Dr Pierre Riviere: 69T, 69B
SHAEF: 62B, 70, 72T
SHAA: 34, 102TR, 111B, 112T
Sirpa-Aiv: Title page, 80T, 80C, 84T, 90T, 94B, 98B, 99T, 100B, 101B, 103T, 104T, 104B, 106B, 107C, 108T, 108B, 110T, 111C, 112B, 117B, 118, 121B, 124T, 124B, 125T, 126T, 127T, 129B, 131T, 135T, 136T, 140B, 141T, 142T, 142C, 142B, 143T, 143B, 144, 146T, 146B, 148C, 148B, 149T, 150, 152T, 152B, 153T, 153B, 154B, 158T, 160T, 161T, 167
Sud Aviation: 103B